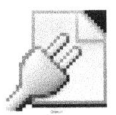

GIN-DOODLETANGLES

Creative ideas for practical gifts

GREAT FOR SENIORS

By: Virginia Burshaw

[ISBN:13-978-1492374763]

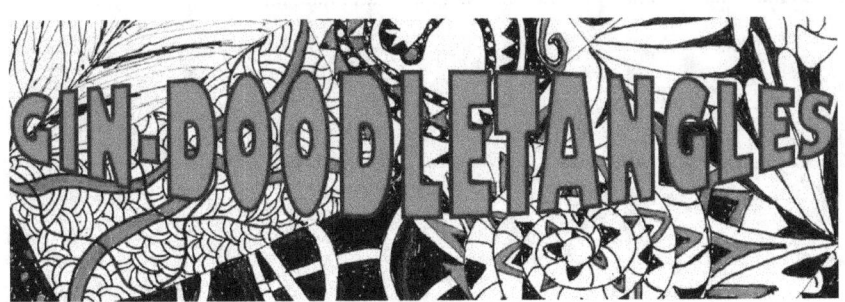

www.gin-doodletangles.com

TABLE OF CONTENTS

About The Author...

GINNY is a vivacious, fun-loving person who loves bling and color

She is always wanting to learn new things to make her life more fulfilling, especially as a senior.

She has been exploring her creative side. Ginny believed she had no creativity in her until she discovered Zentangles.

She has since re-named them Gin-doodletangles and began learning all the different ways they can be used.

It has become an exciting adventure into a creative world she never knew existed in herself.

Ginny invites people of every age to explore this easy- to- learn, art form, especially seniors who have seemingly lost their zest for life.

This is truly a wonderful meditative way to escape into another world of color, shapes and possibilities.

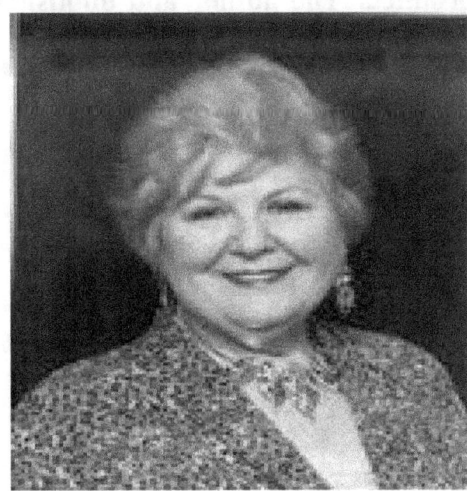

PUBLISHERS NOTES

Paperback Edition

DEDICATION

This book is dedicated in remembrance to my son Ronald William Tweed, who passed away in 1981. He is my inspiration to what I am doing now, and with joy and happiness I desire to bring inspiration to all who have lost a loved one and to show that there is something we can contribute to the world. I suggest trying to do some Zentangles to relieve stress, worry and any other emotional problems you might be going through... Happy Zentangles to you!

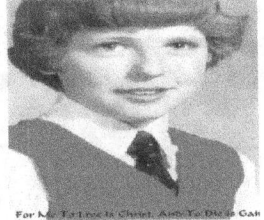

For Me, To Live Is Christ, And To Die Is Gain

OLD PURSE COVERED WITH DOODLE TANGLE

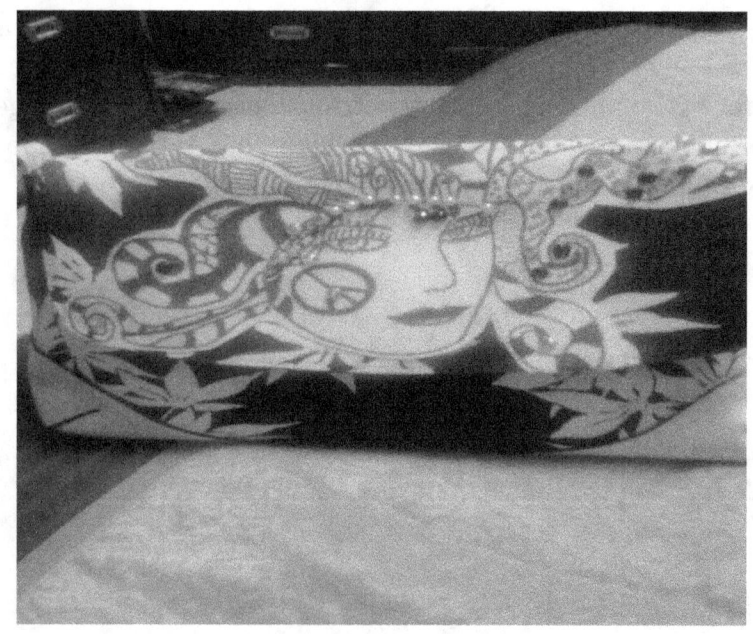

CHAPTER 1-

Enter Chapter 1 Content.

Supplies to use :Sharpie Markers & Pens, Artist Pens, Pencils, Canvas Sheets, Alymer Glue, No Sew Glue, Jewel It Glue, Artist Drawing Pad, Beads. Use your imagination , let it soar.

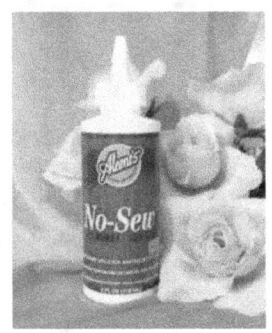
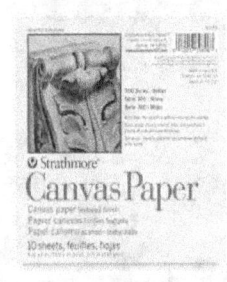
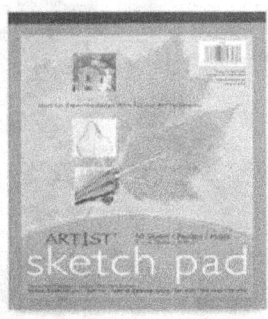

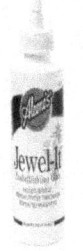
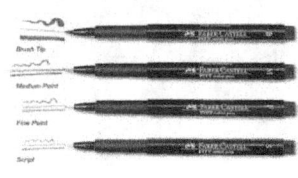
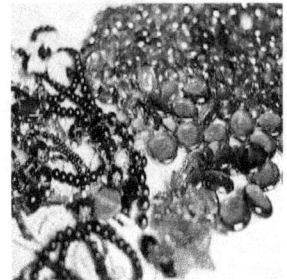

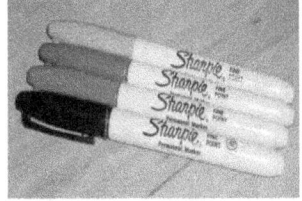
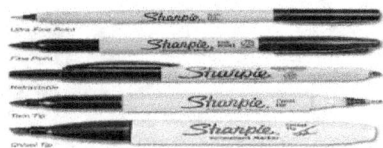

CHAPTER 2- USED ITEMS

IDEAS FOR USED ARTICLES

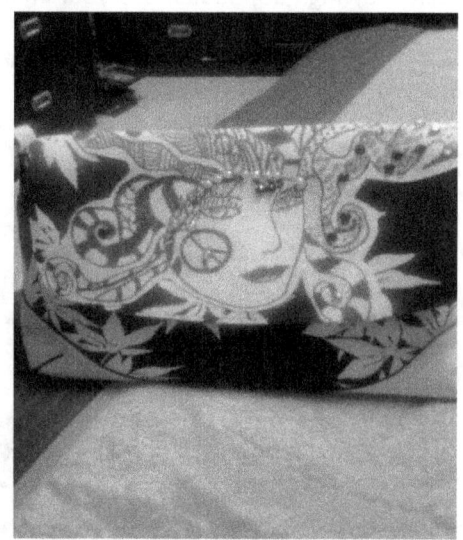

RECOVERED OLD PURSE

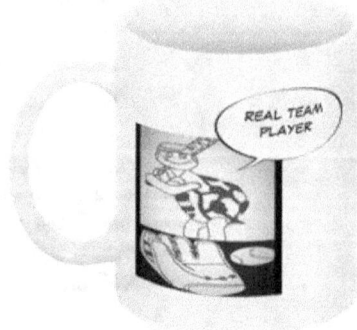

CHAPTER 3-

ASSORTED CUSTOM NOTE CARDS: **MUG**

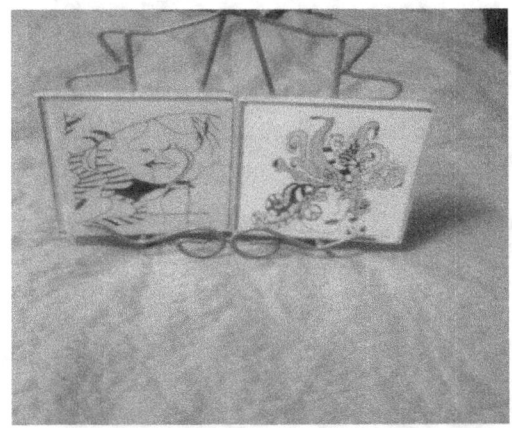

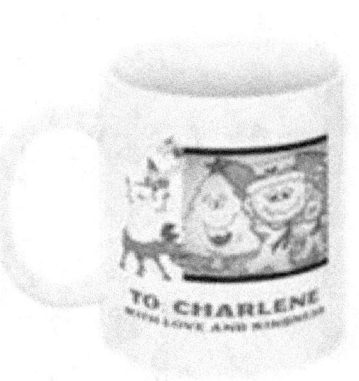

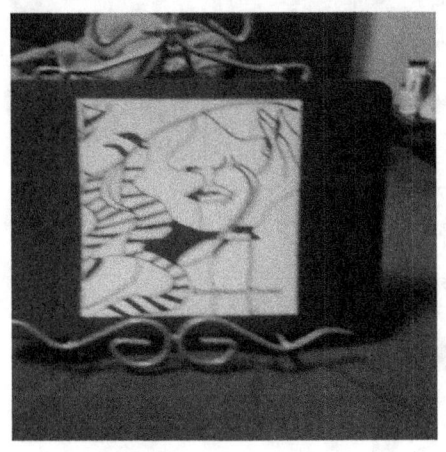

Designs on Mouse-pad

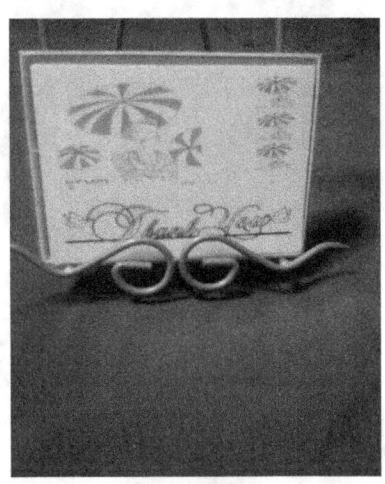

Note Cards

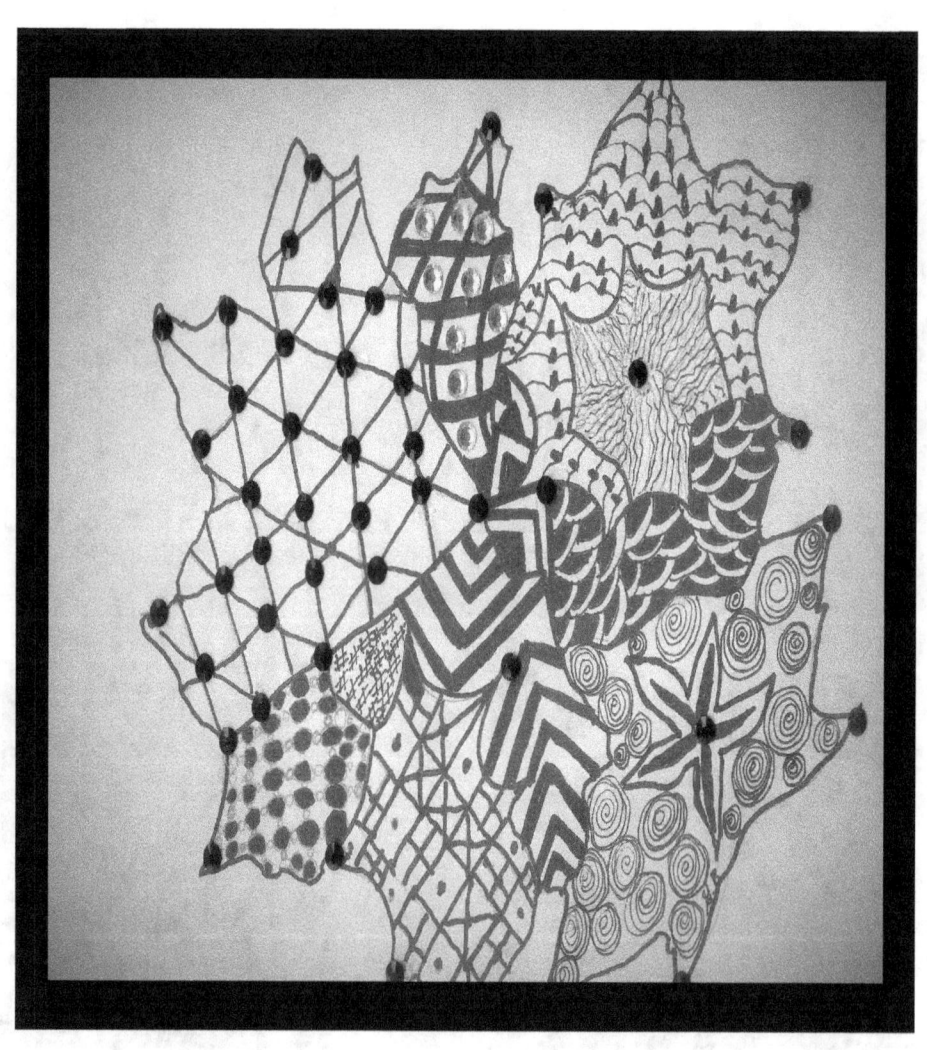

AUTUMN LEAVES

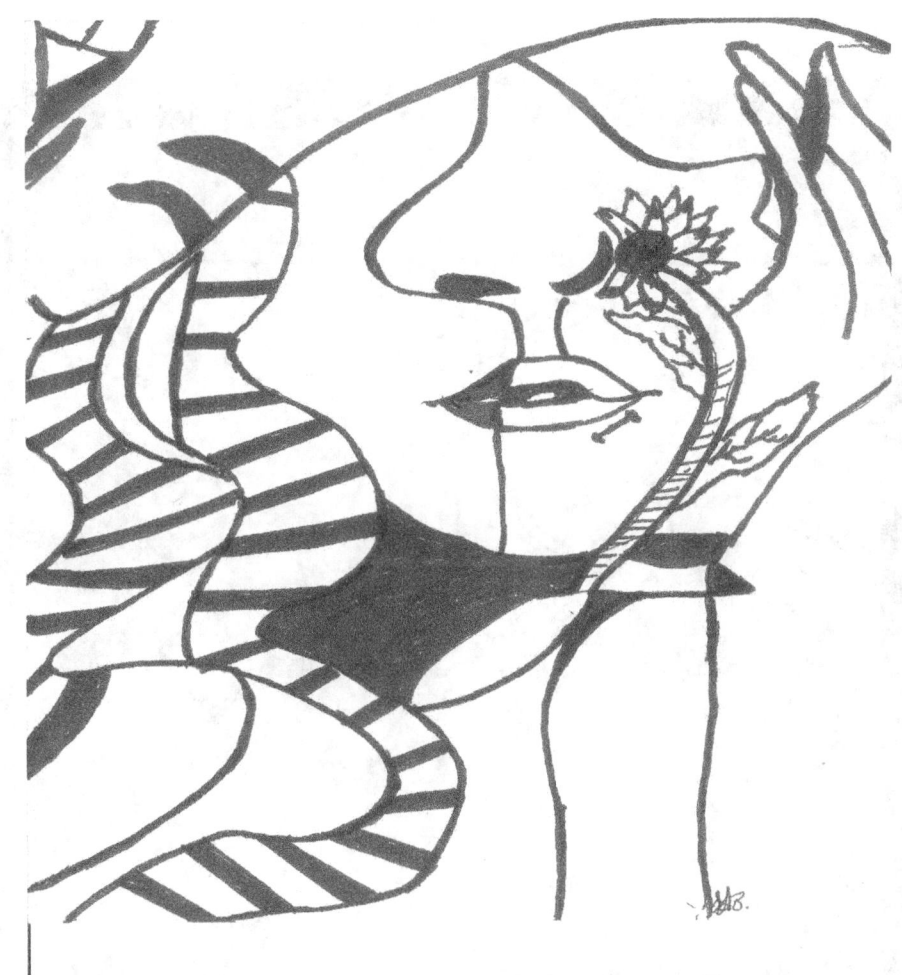

European Twist

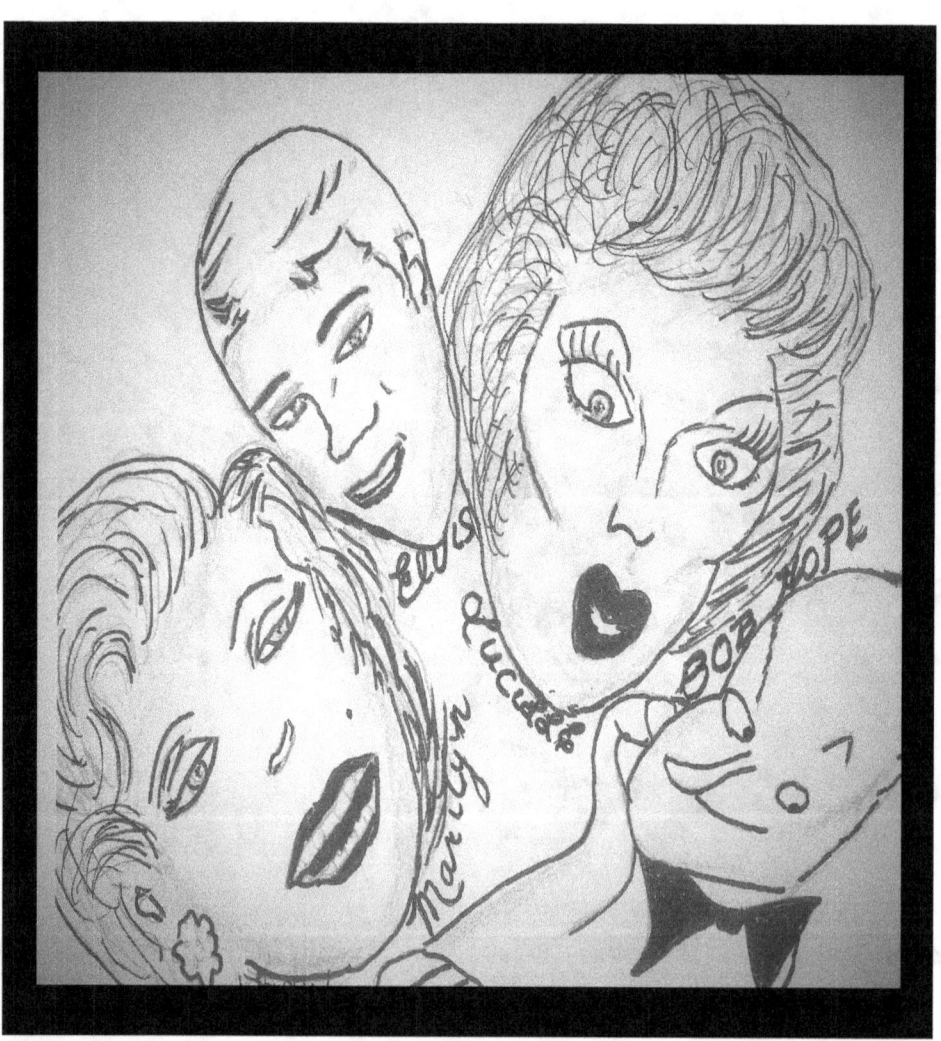

The Foursome

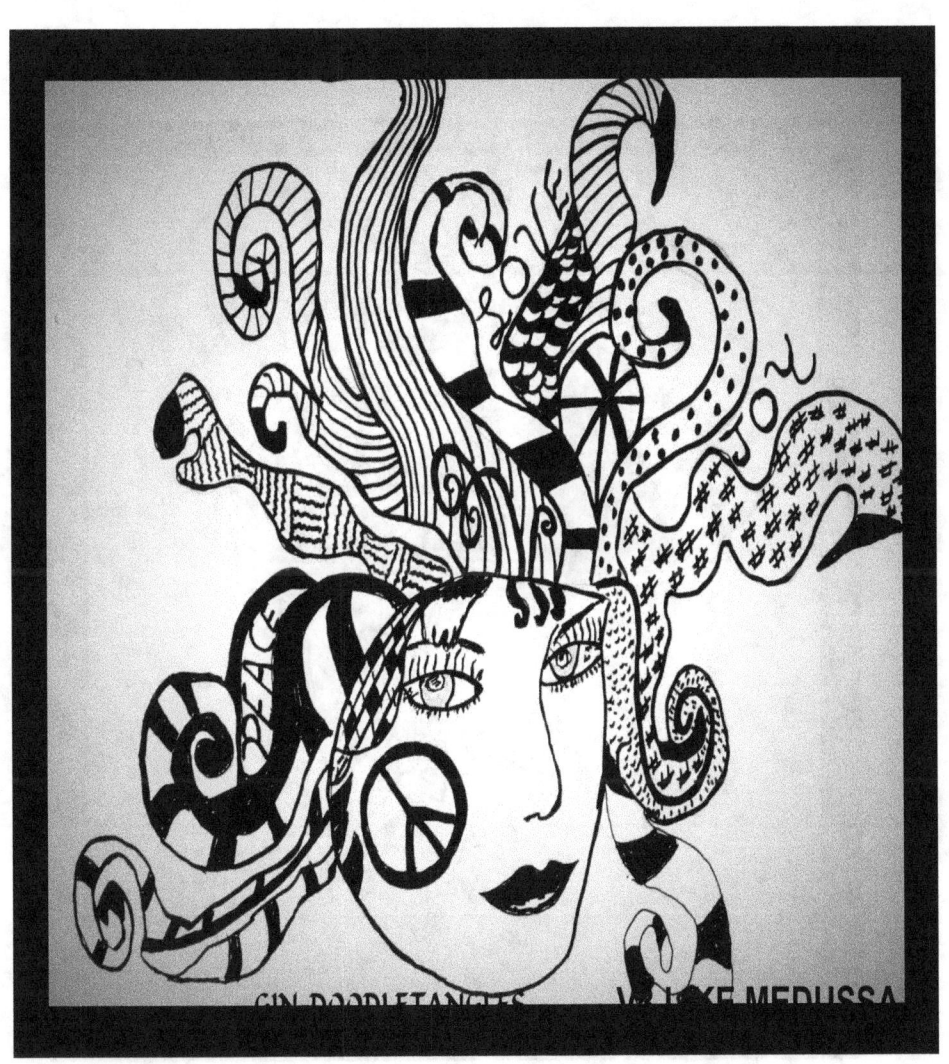

LIKE MEDUSSA

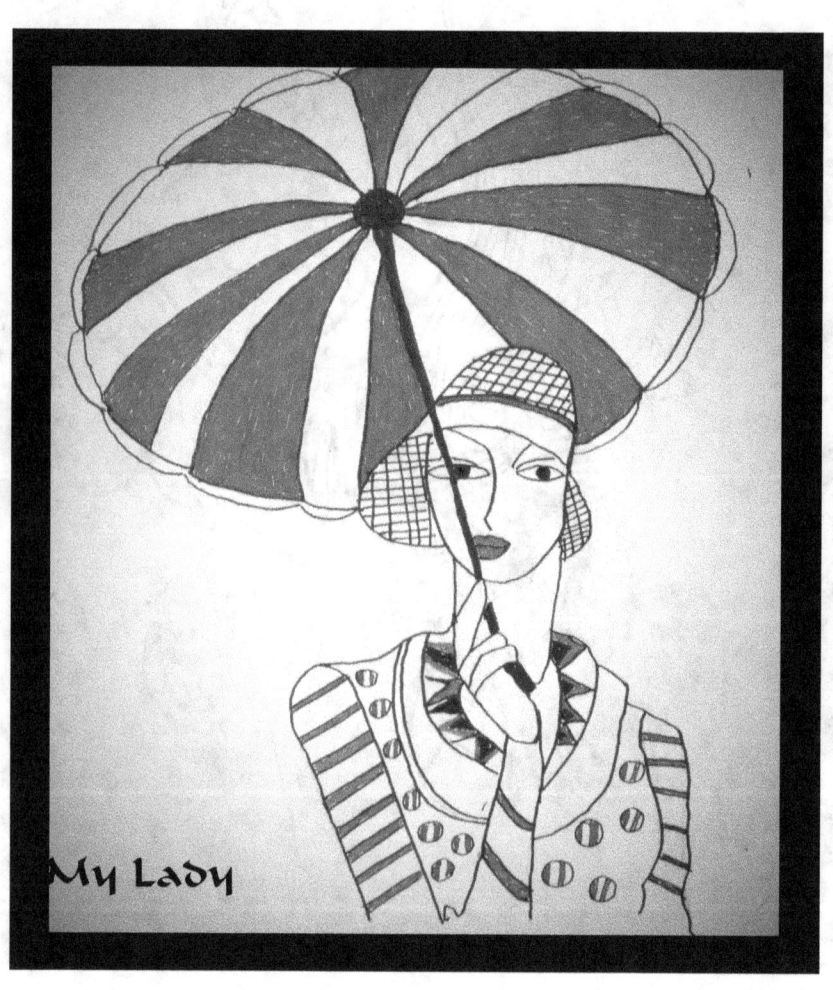

My Lady

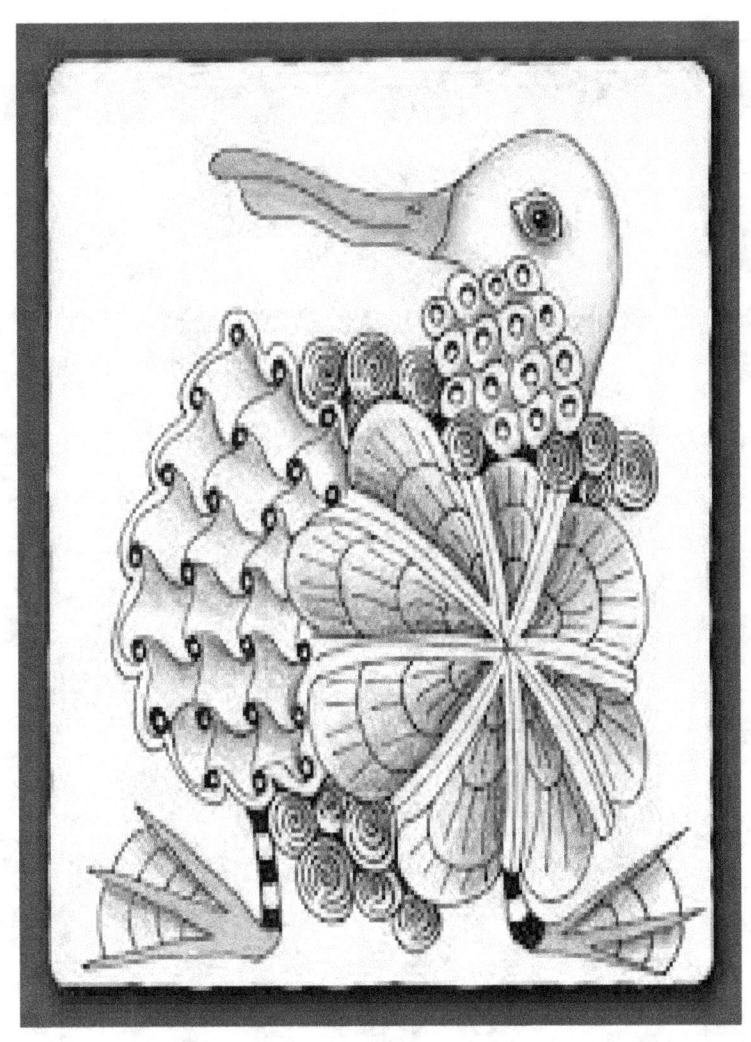

DUCK

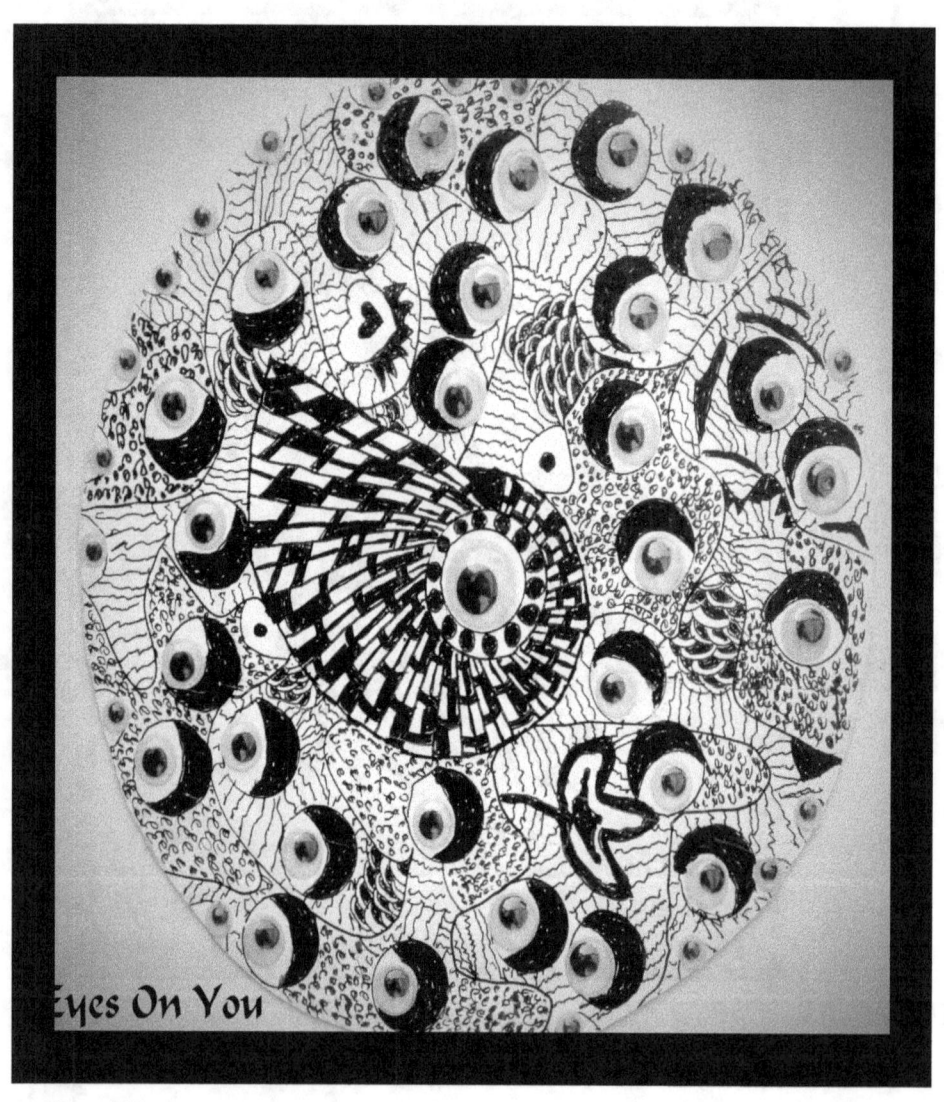

Eyes On You

EYES ON YOU

My Hand

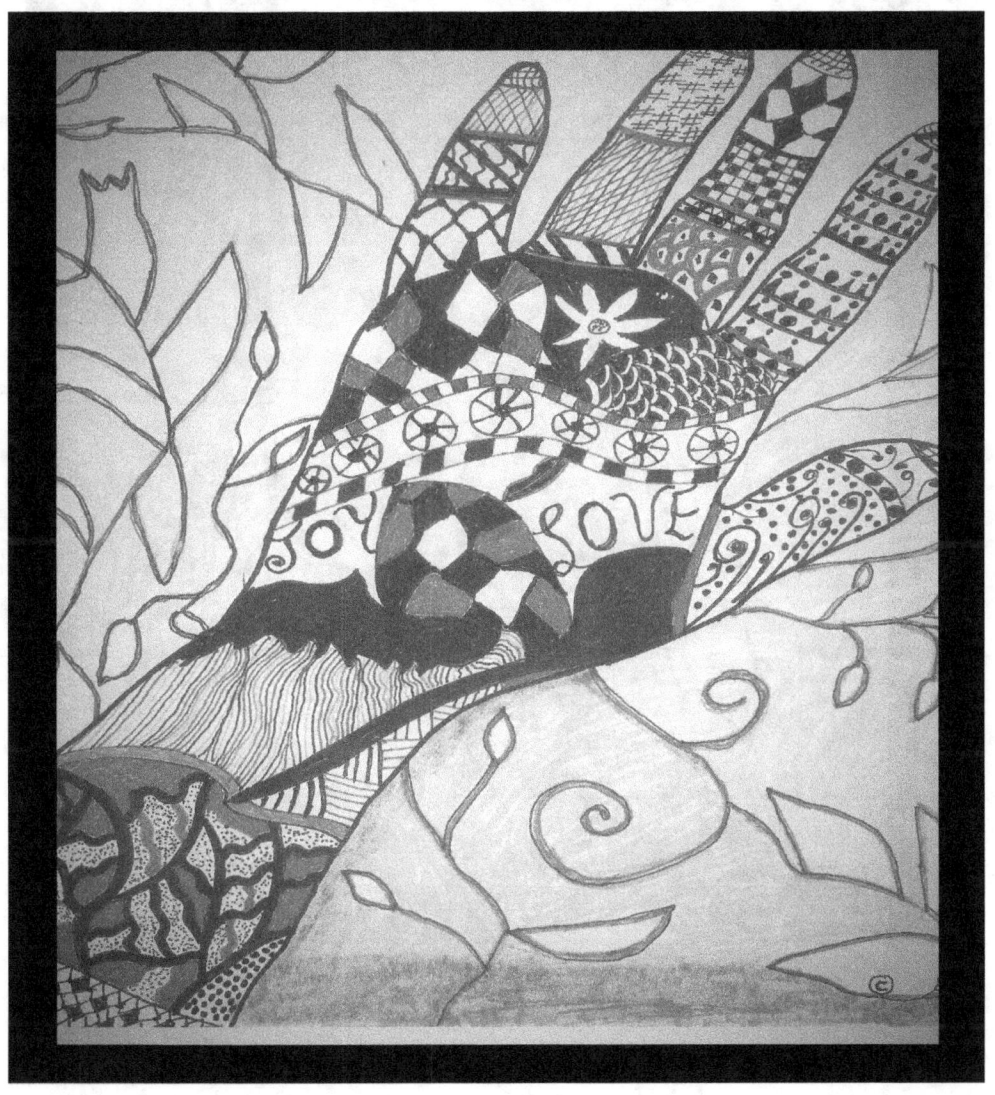

Space Flower

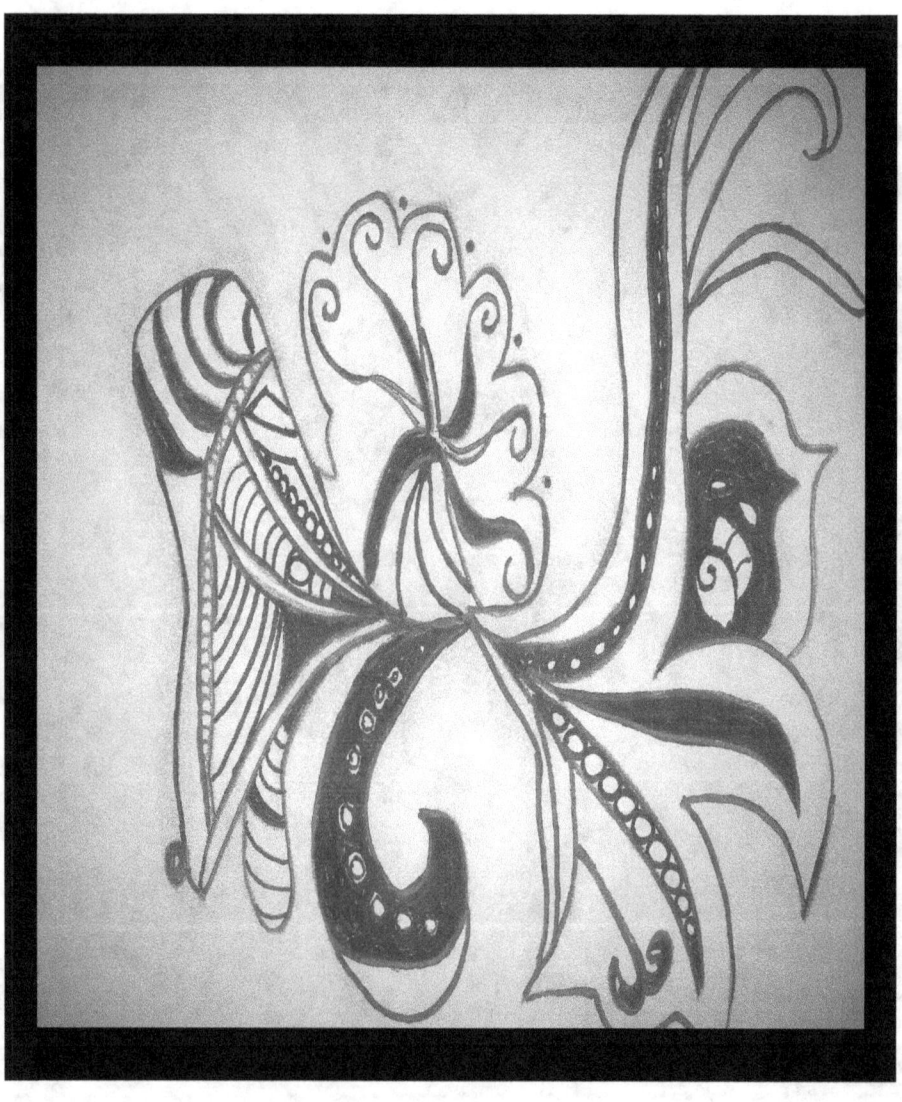

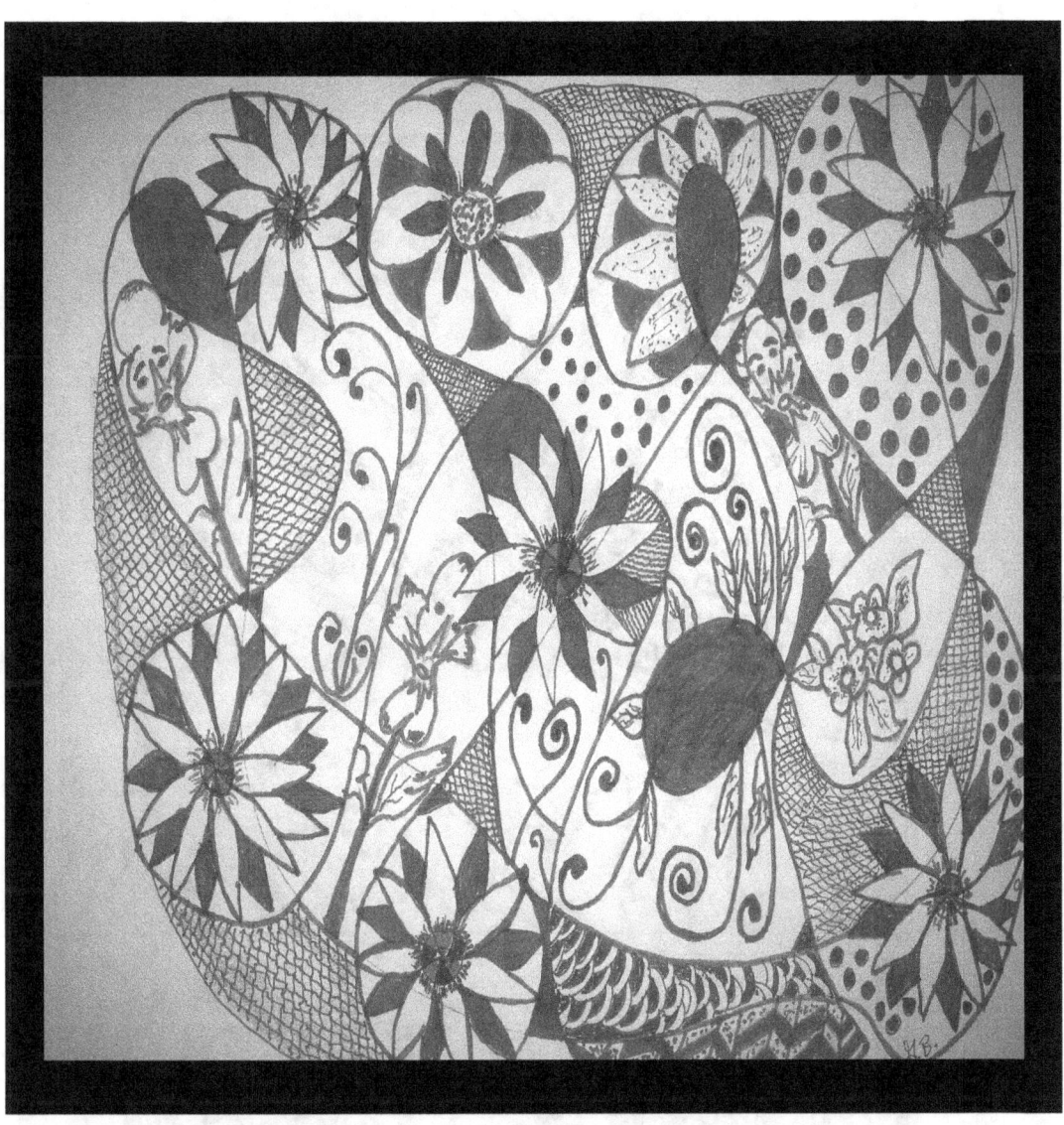

Bloomers

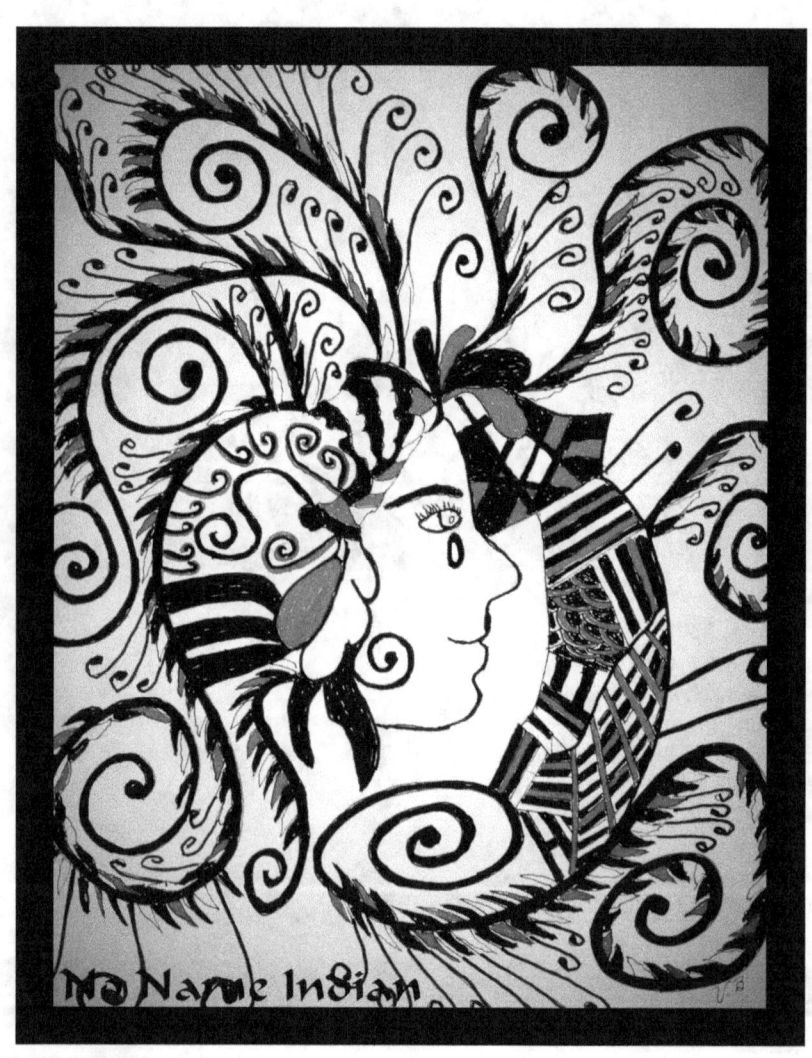

NO NAME INDIAN

What do you See

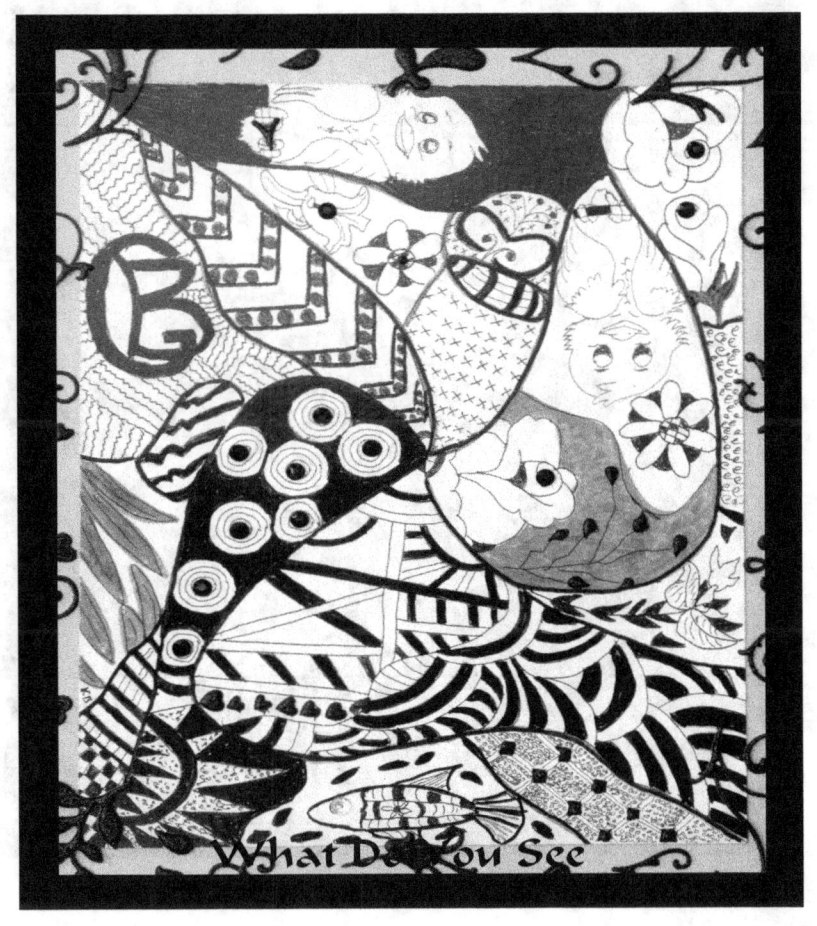

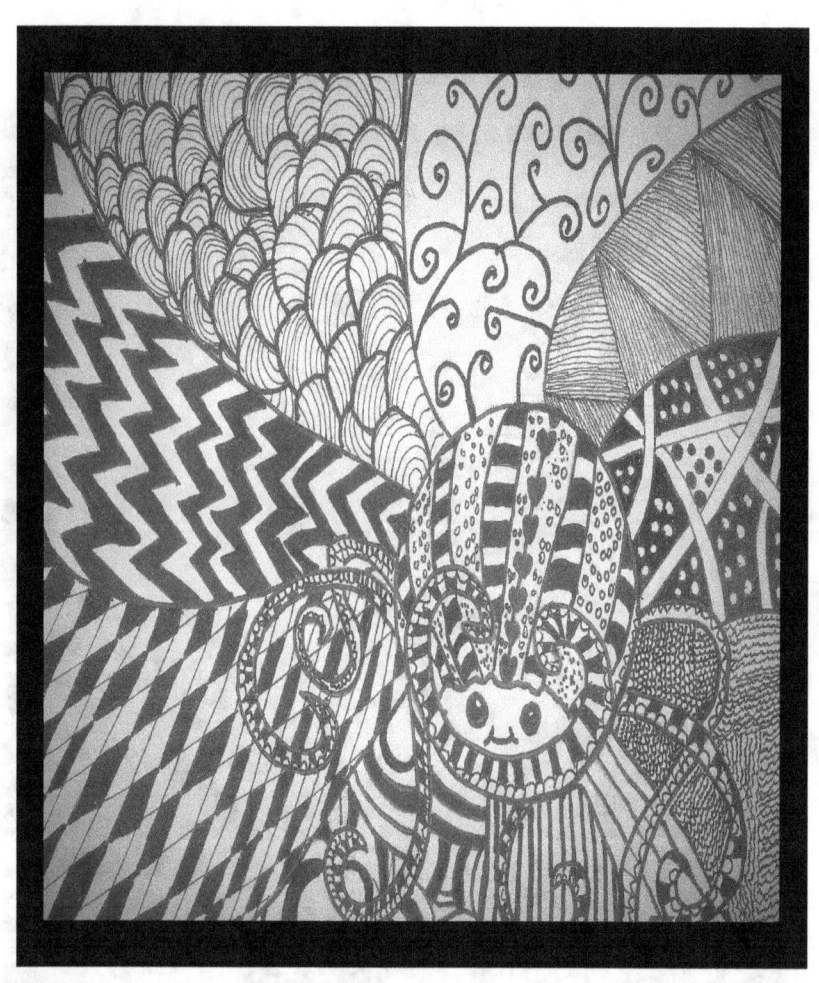

MOMMA SPIDER

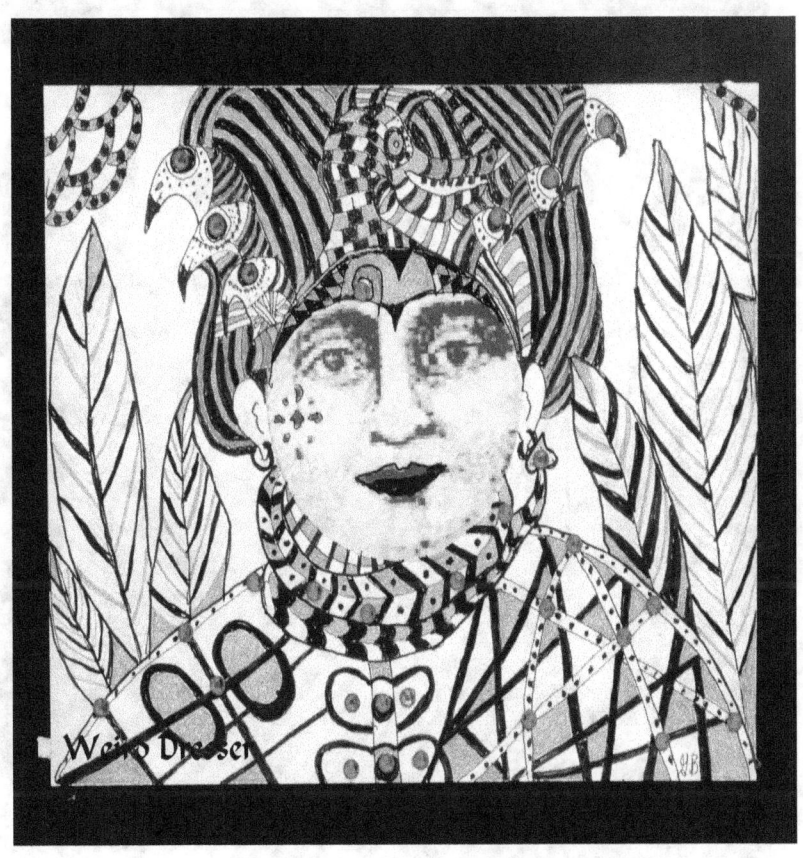

Weird Dresser

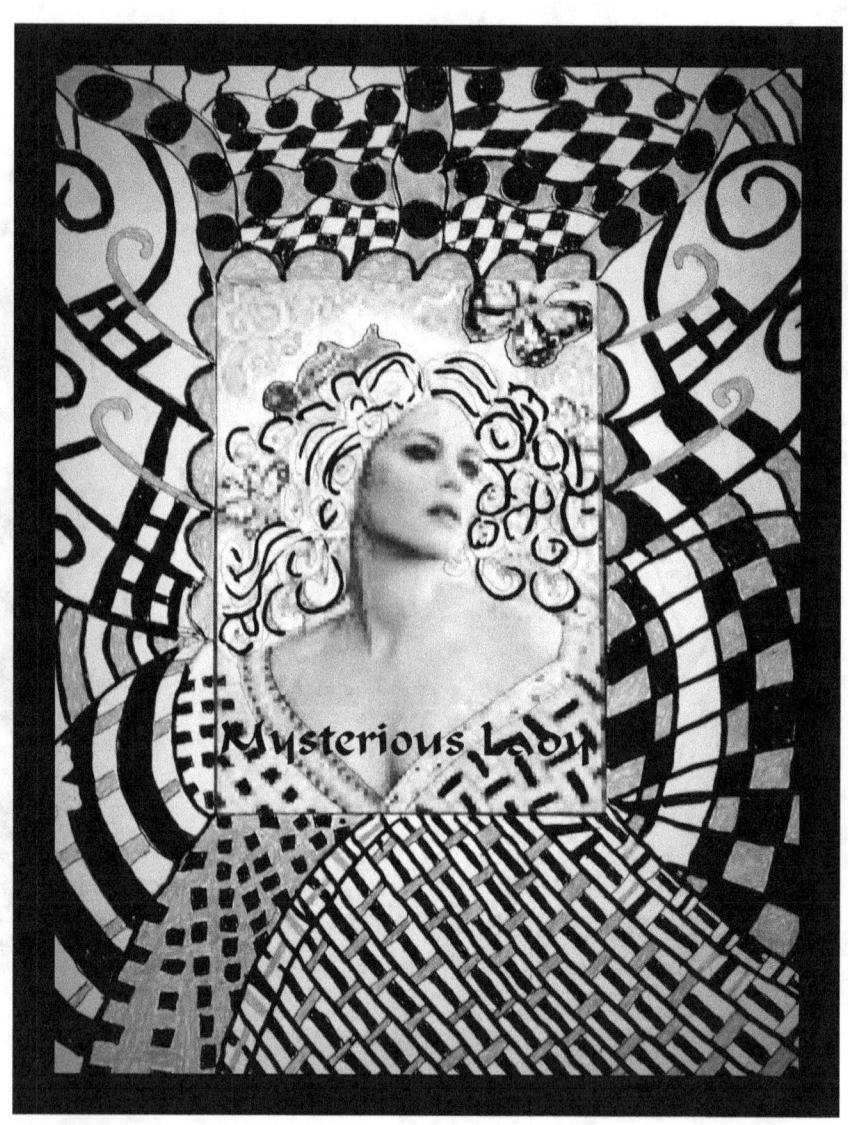

Mysterious Lady

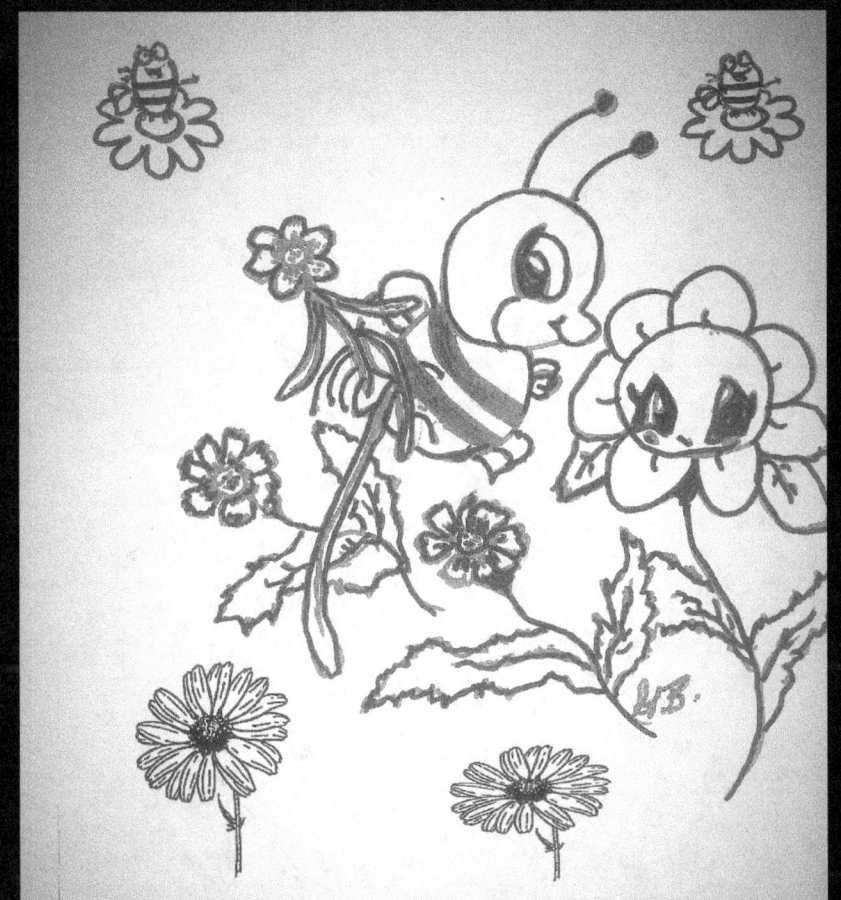

BEE MINE

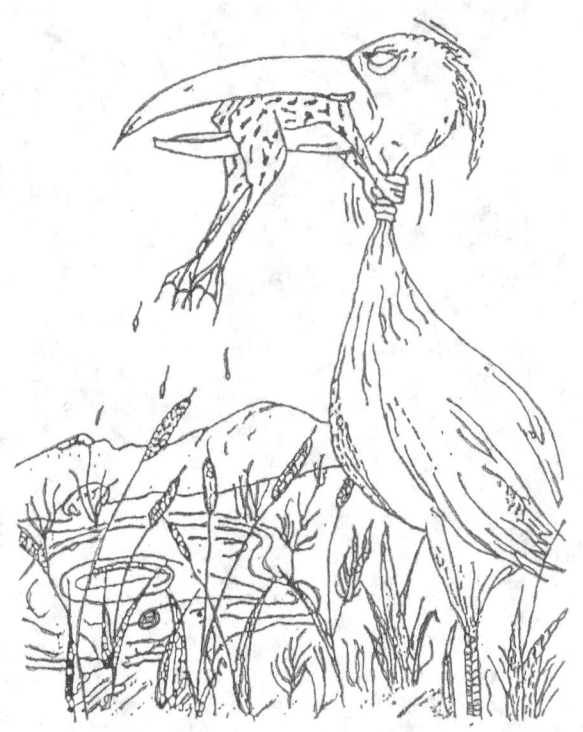

Don't EVER give up!

HOW TO MAKE A ZENTANGLE

A Zentangle is an abstract drawing created using repetitive patterns. It is usually structured within a certain shape. Drawing a Zentangle is entertaining, relaxing, and a great way to express yourself creatively.

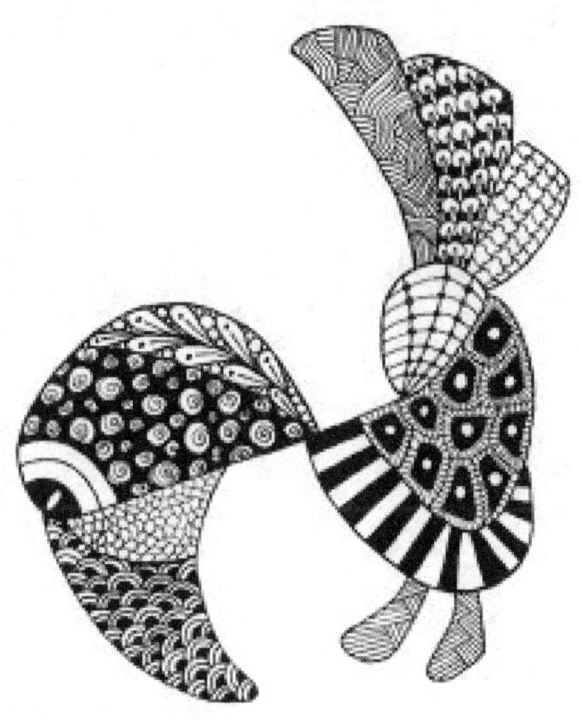

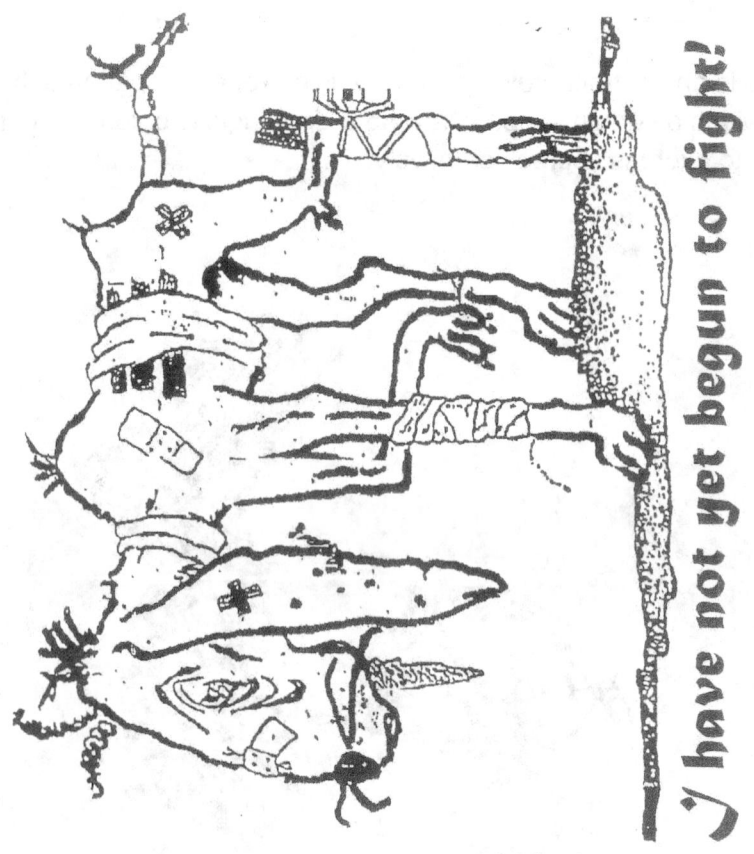

♩ I have not yet begun to fight!

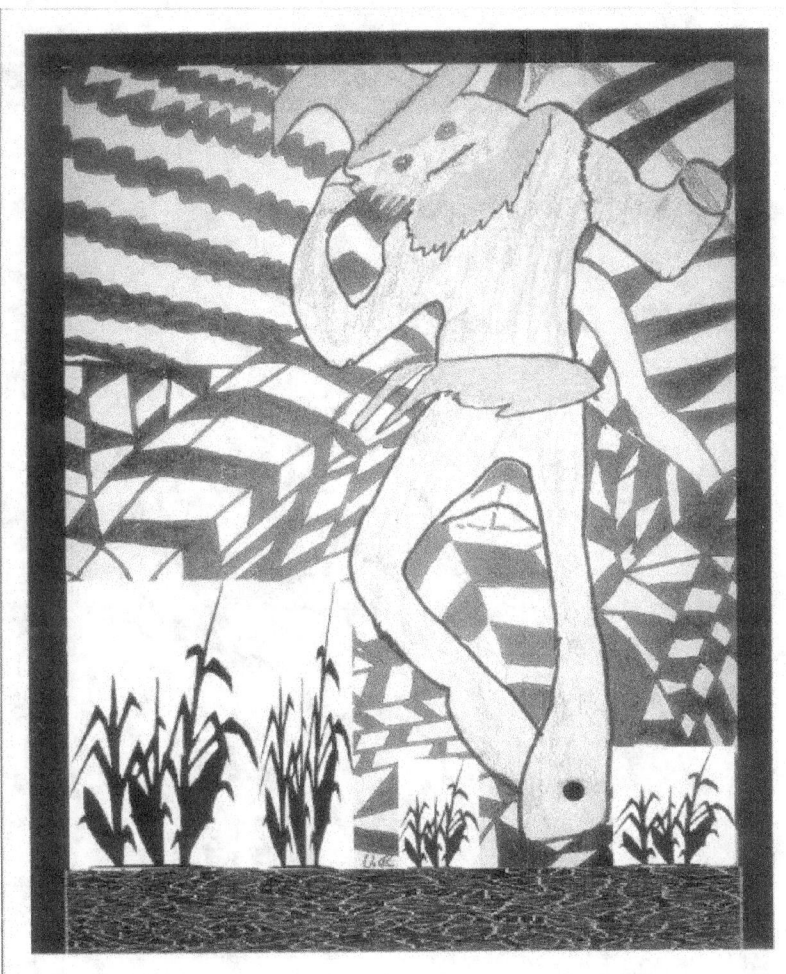

SCARECROW

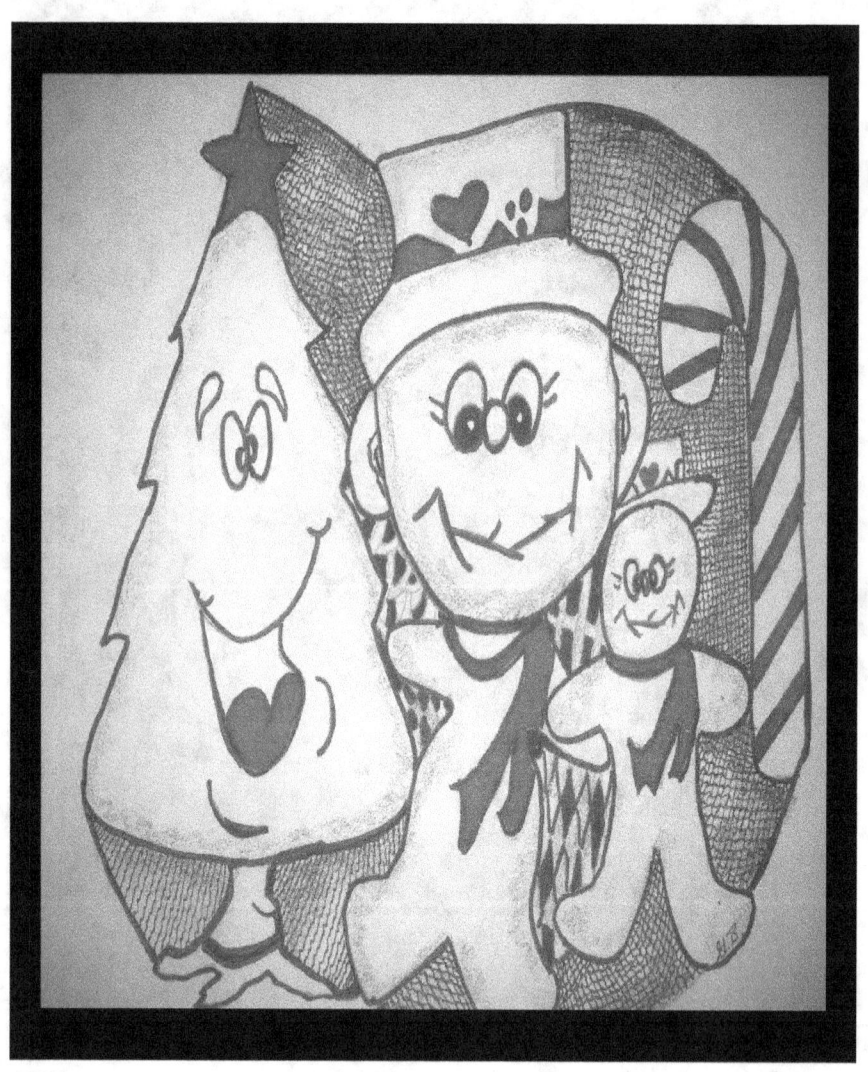

SNOWMAN

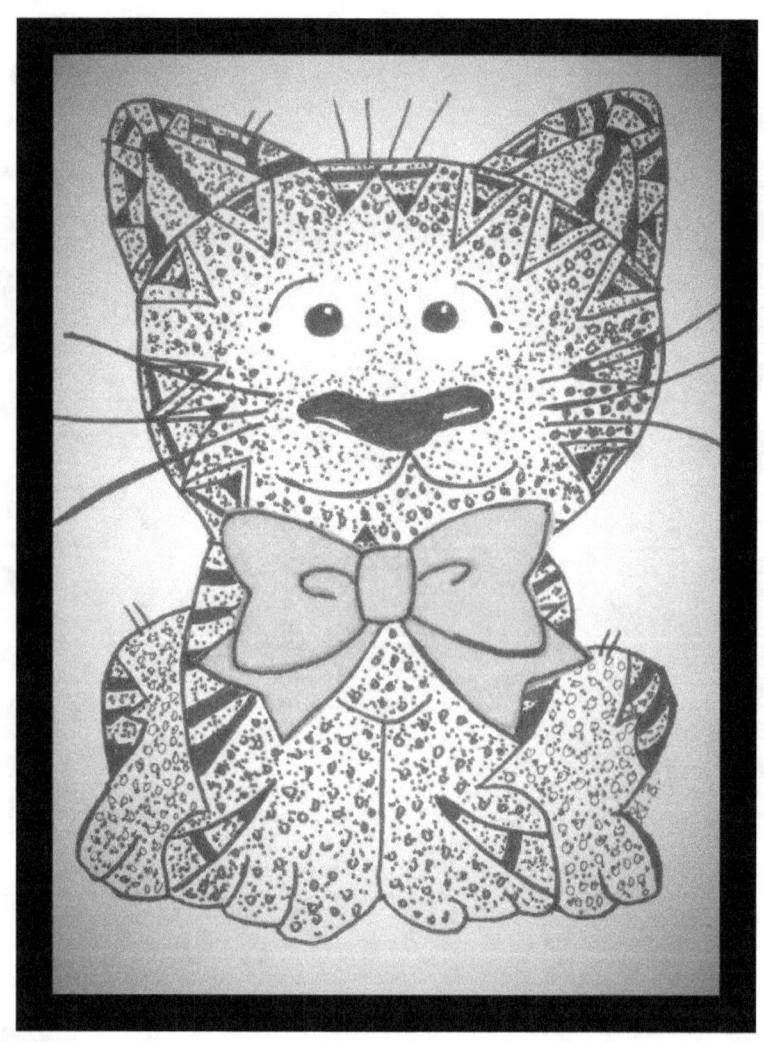

SCAREDY CAT

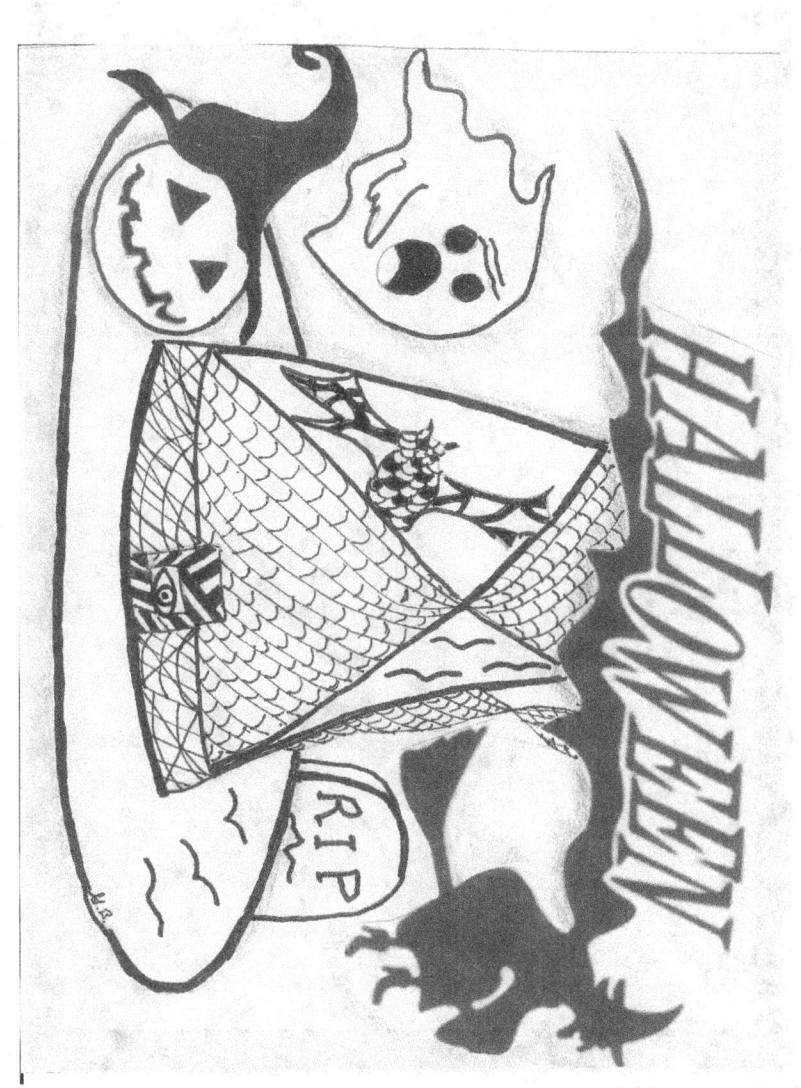

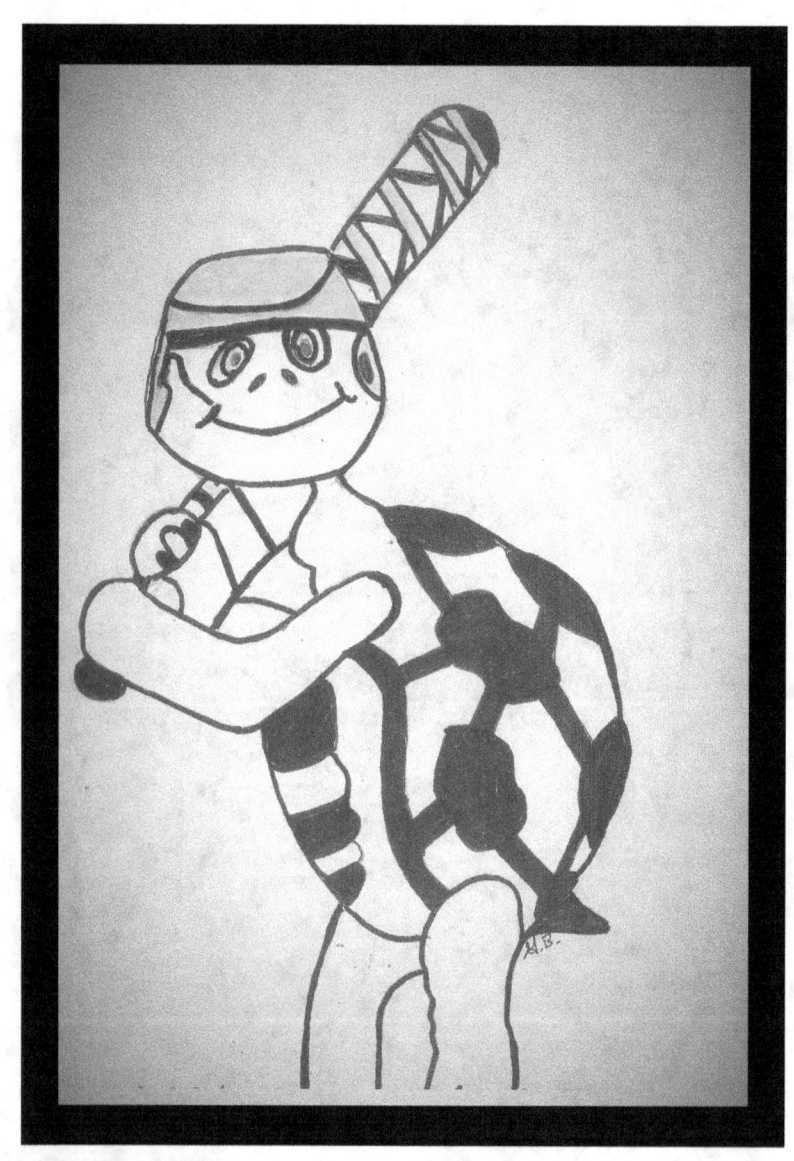

REAL TEAM PLAYER

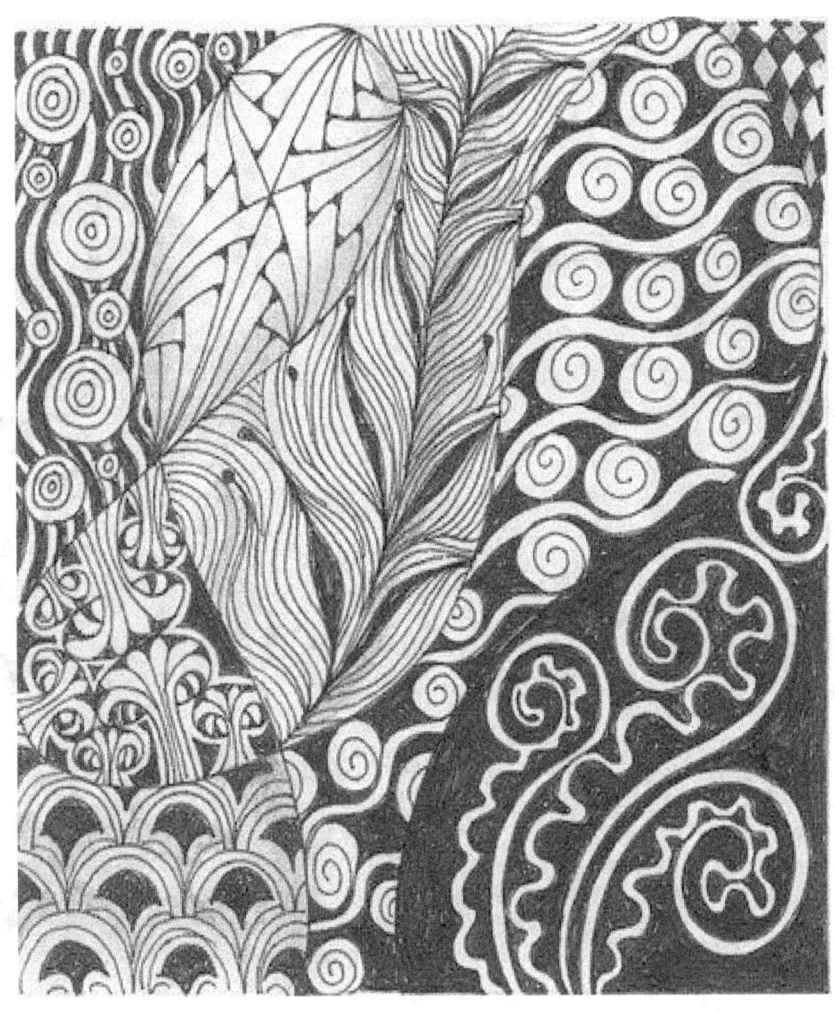

RING OF FIRE

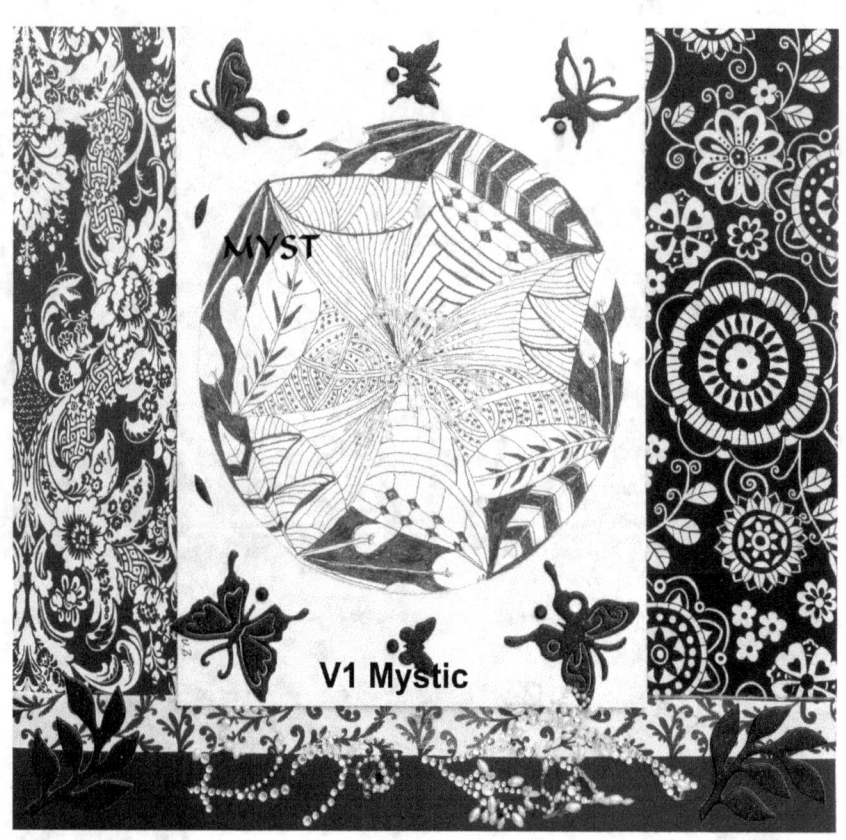

MYSTIC

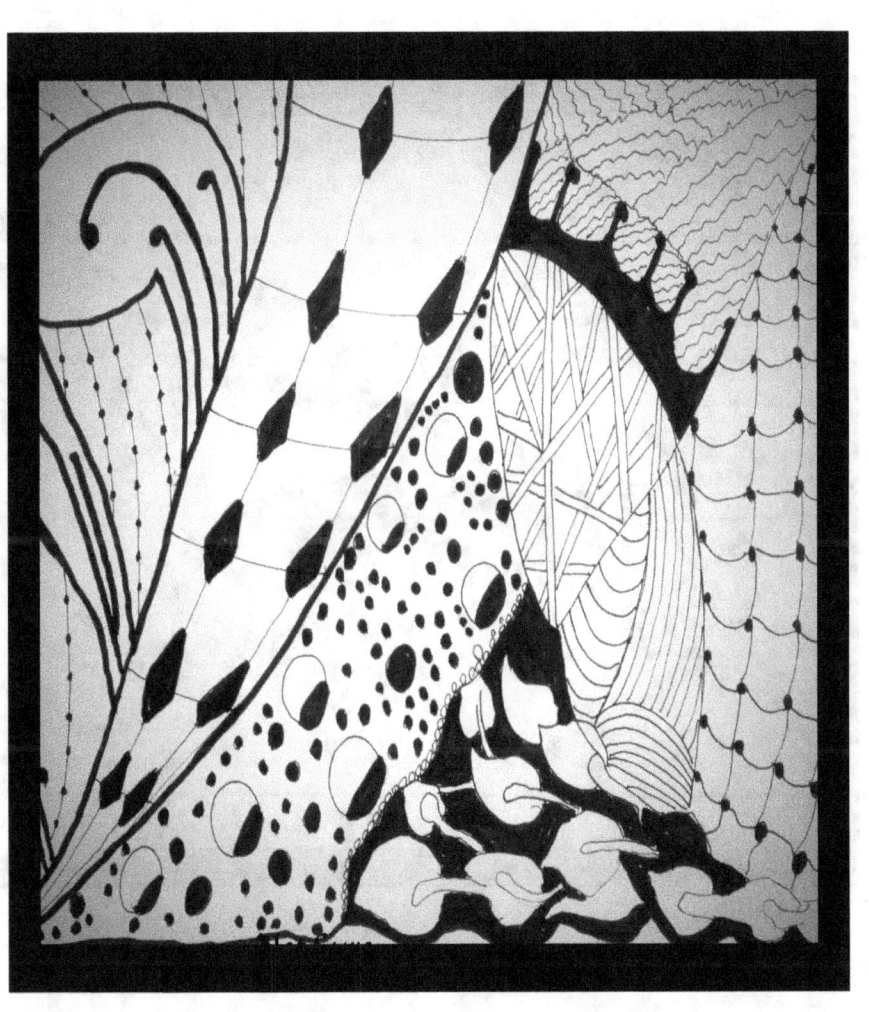

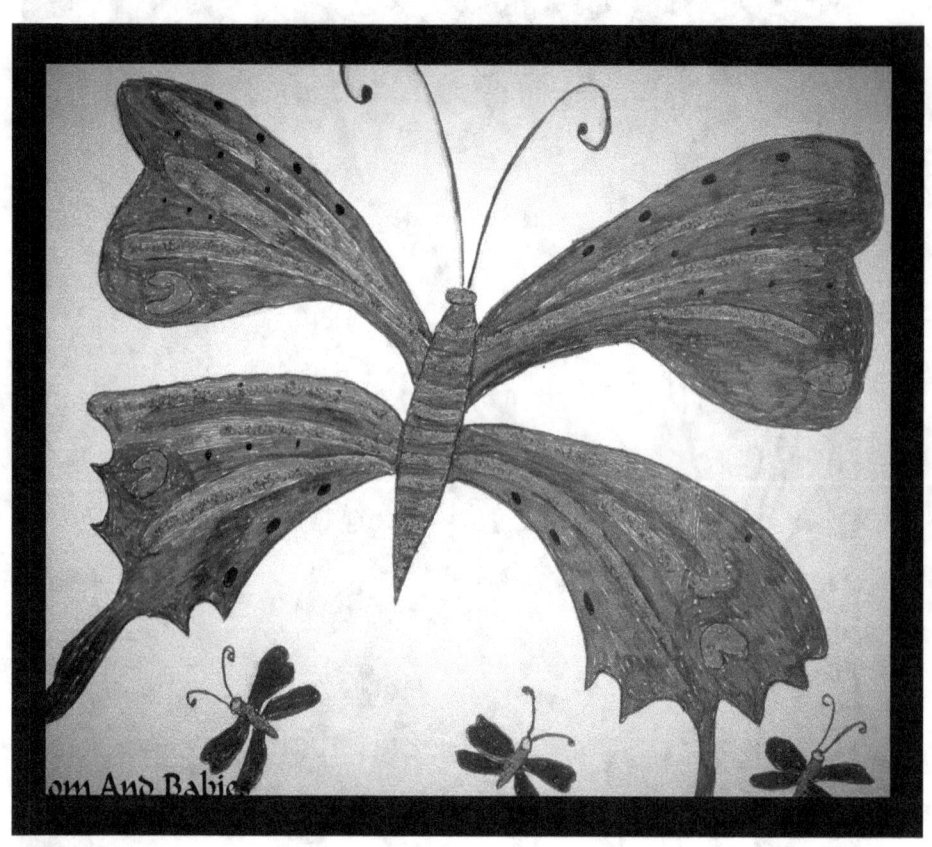

MOM AND BABIES

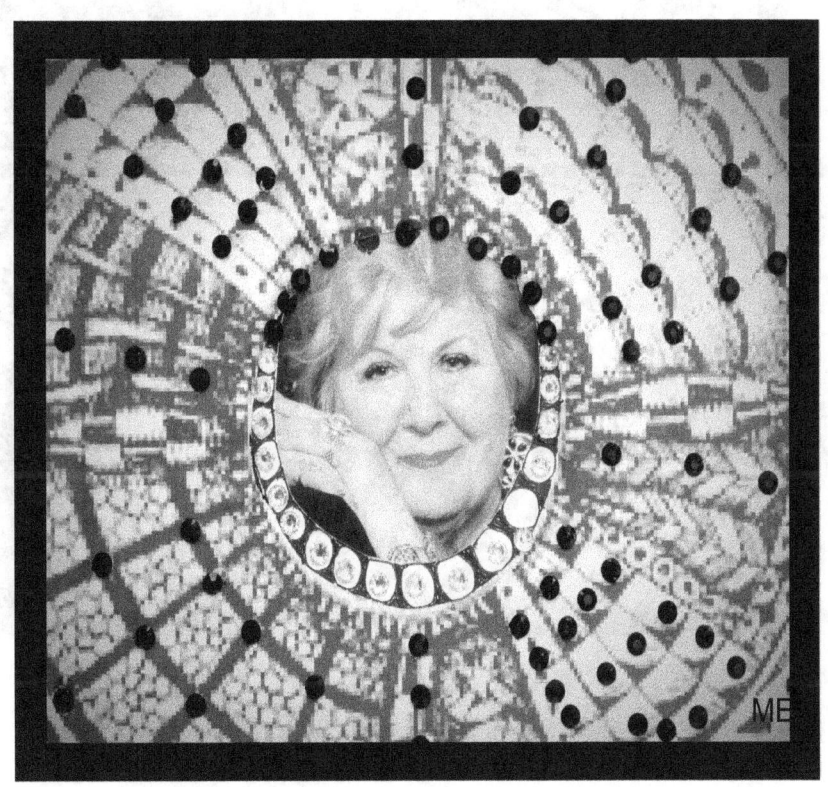

PUT PICTURE OF LOVED ONE OR AN ANIMAL

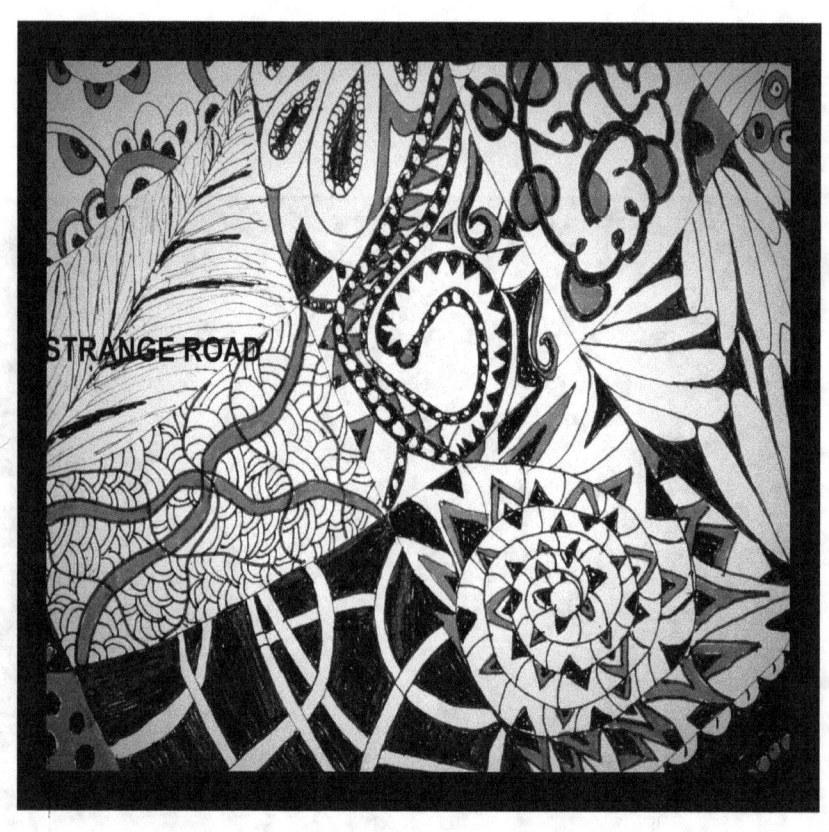

STRANGE ROAD

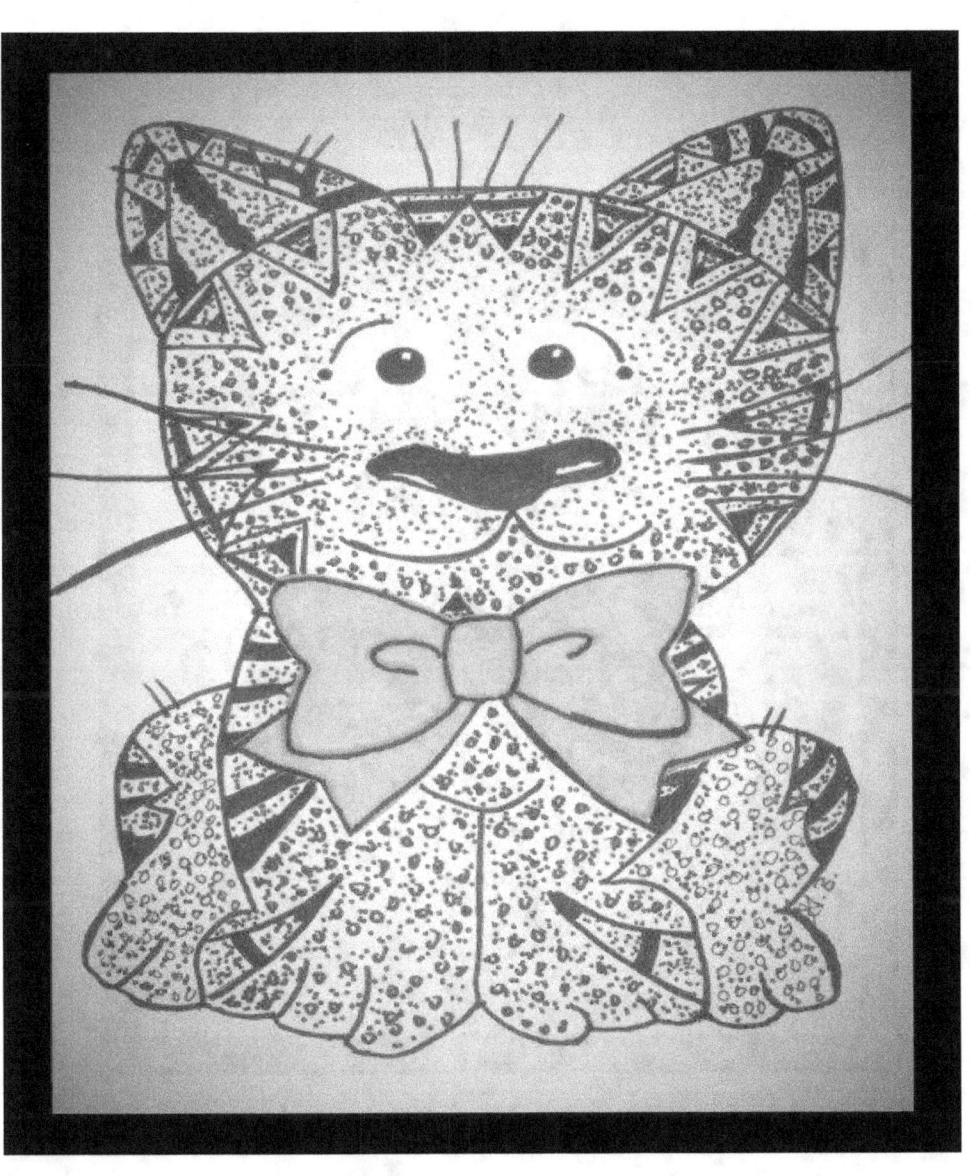

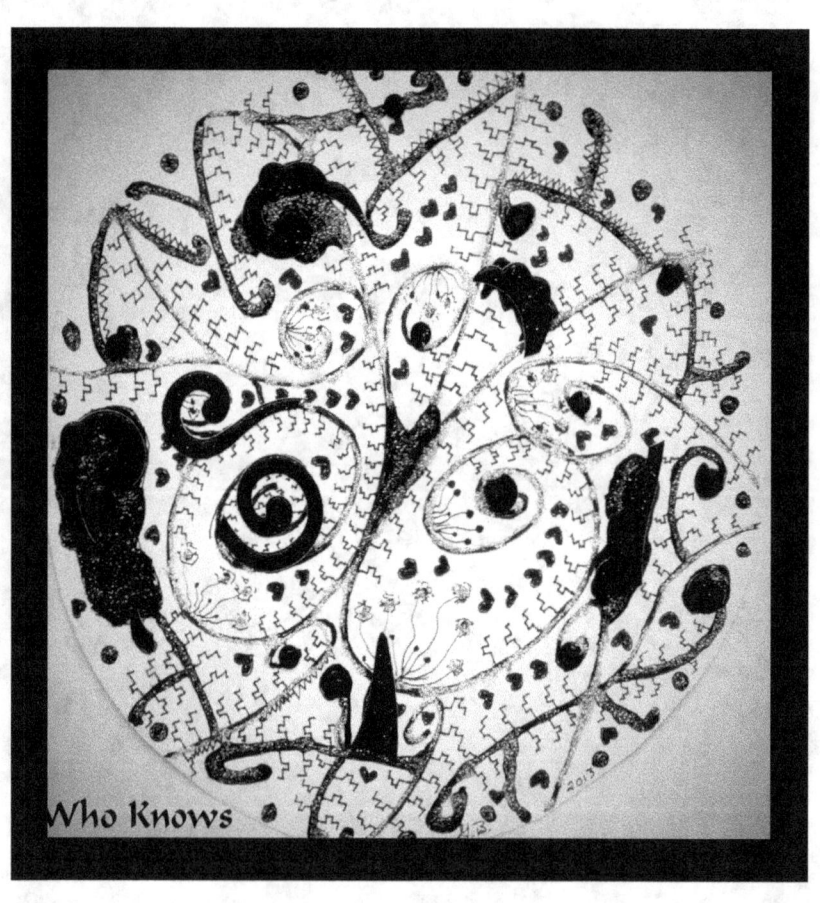

StepsHow to Make a Zentangle

A Zentangle is an abstract drawing created using repetitive patterns. It is usually structured within a certain shape. Drawing a Zentangle is entertaining, relaxing, and a great way to express yourself creatively.

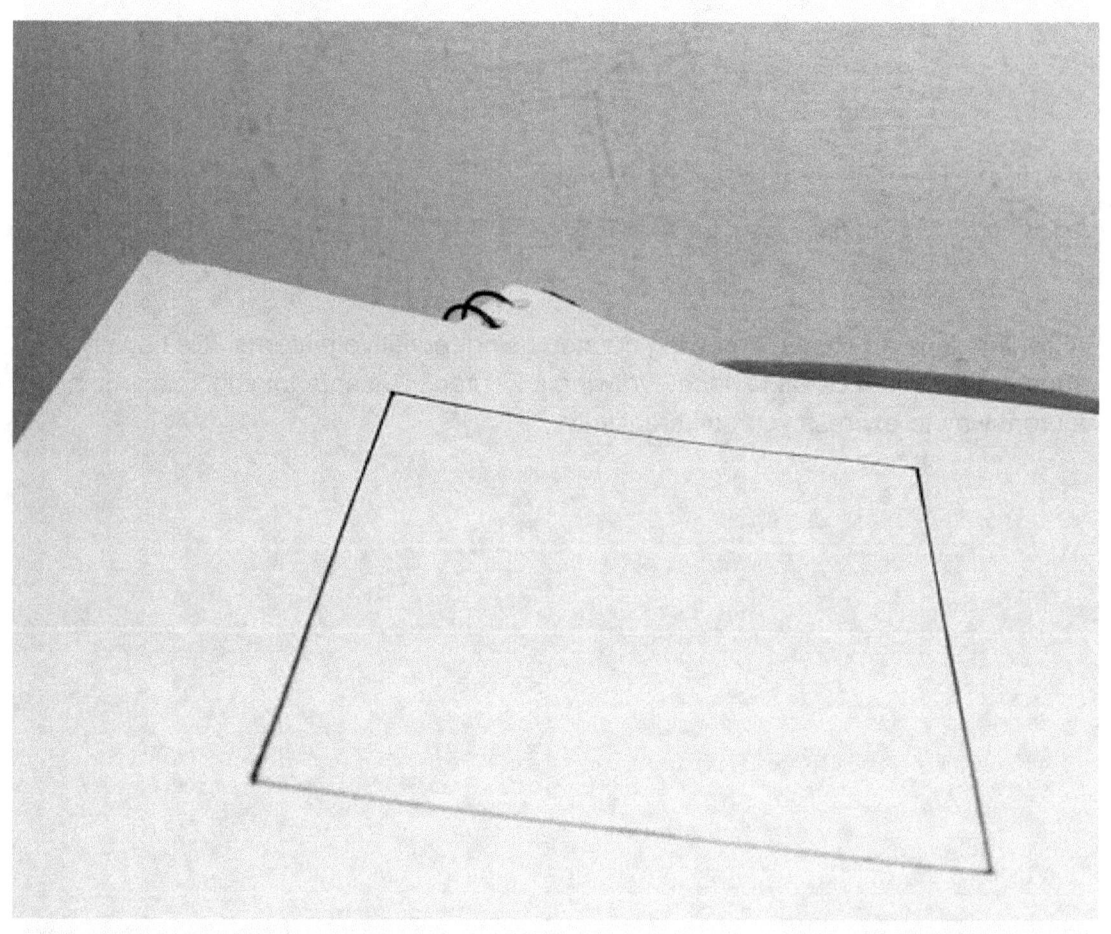

1

Draw a border outlining the shape of your Zentangle. It is very common to use a square shape. The shape is usually relatively small (about 3 inches wide) as most Zentangles are drawn in one sitting.

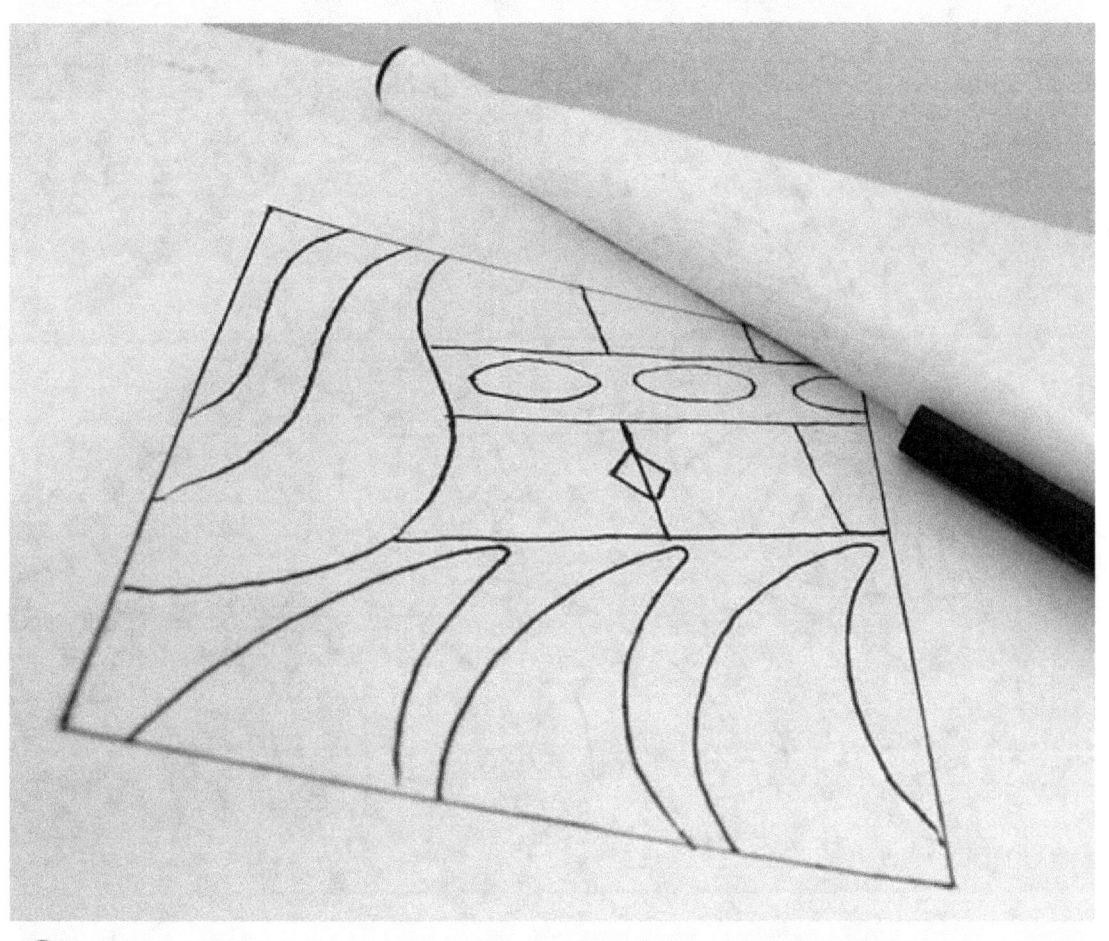

2

Draw strings using a pencil. Strings are lines that divide the shape into individual sections.

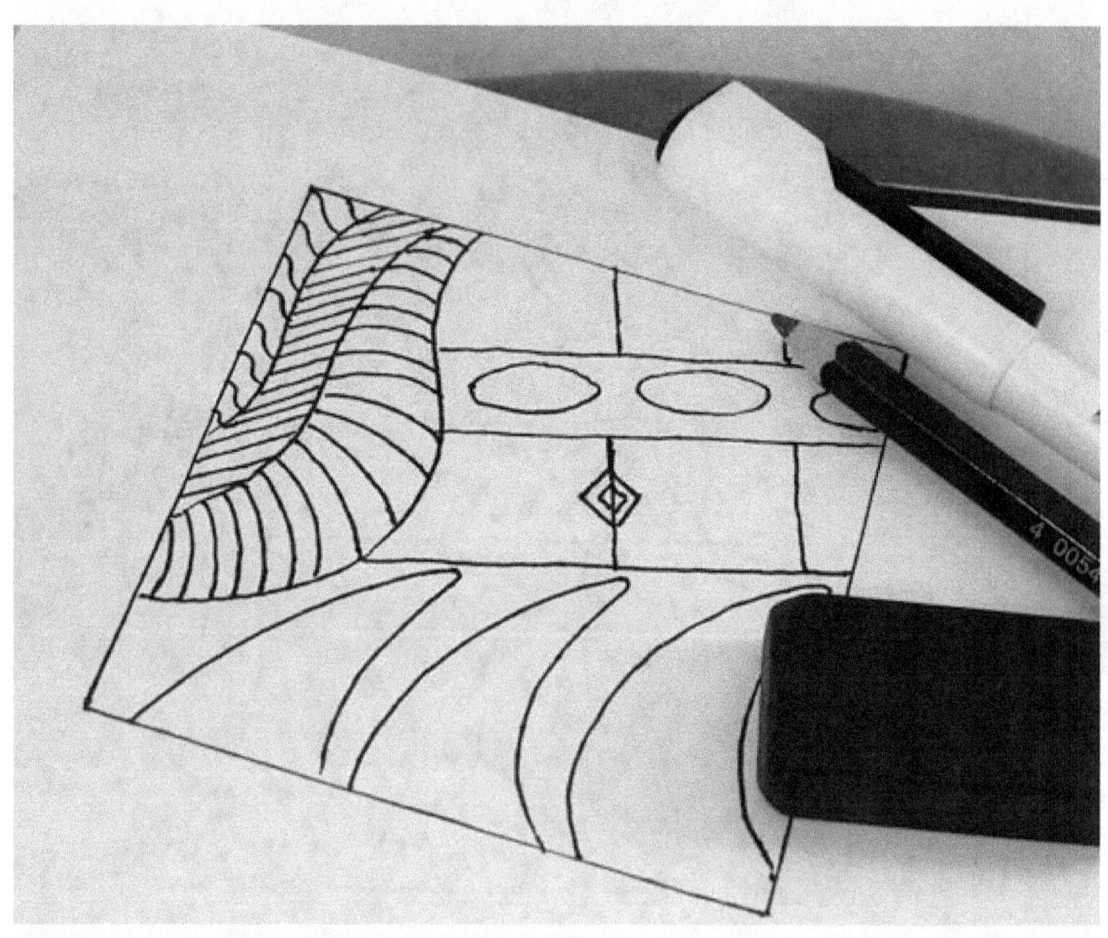

3

Fill one section with a repetitive pattern. Don't spend too much time
planning the pattern, just draw.

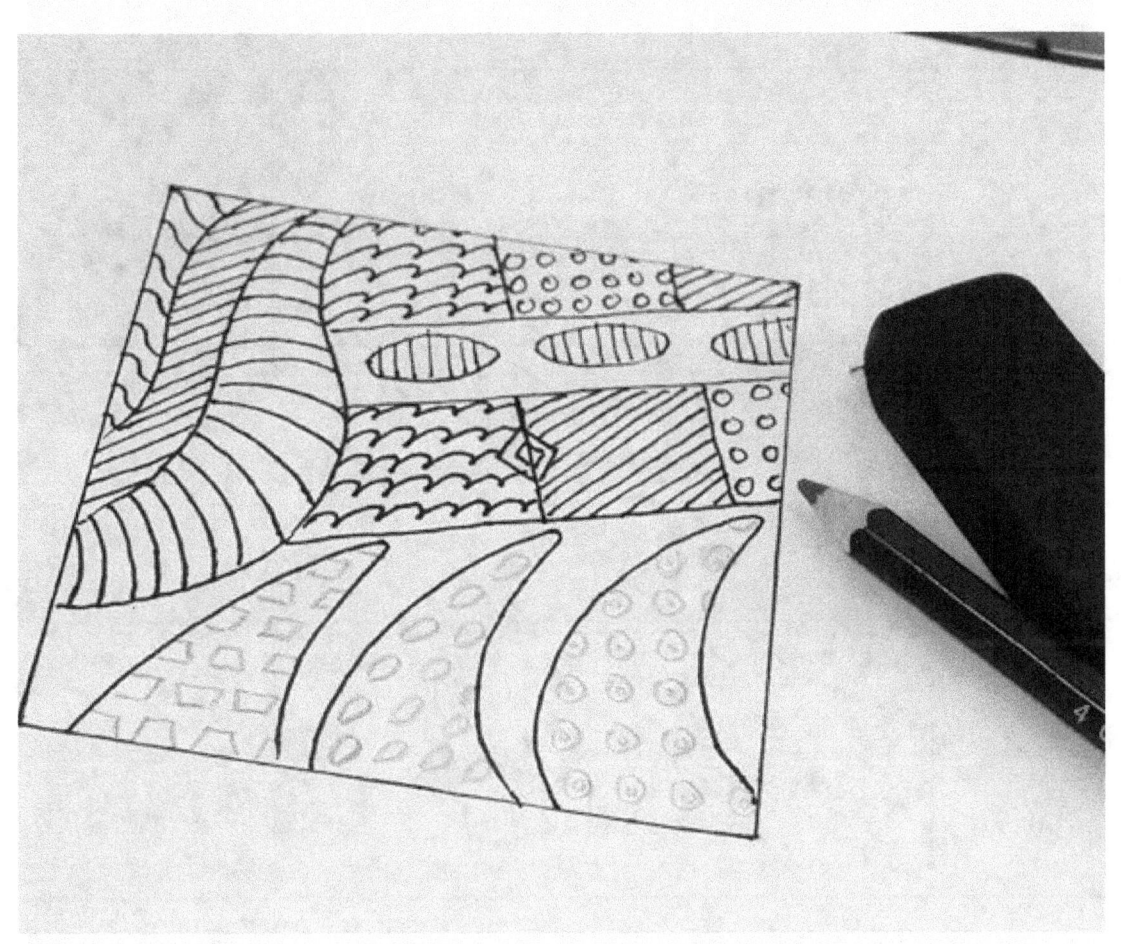

4

Repeat with each section. Change the pattern with each section.

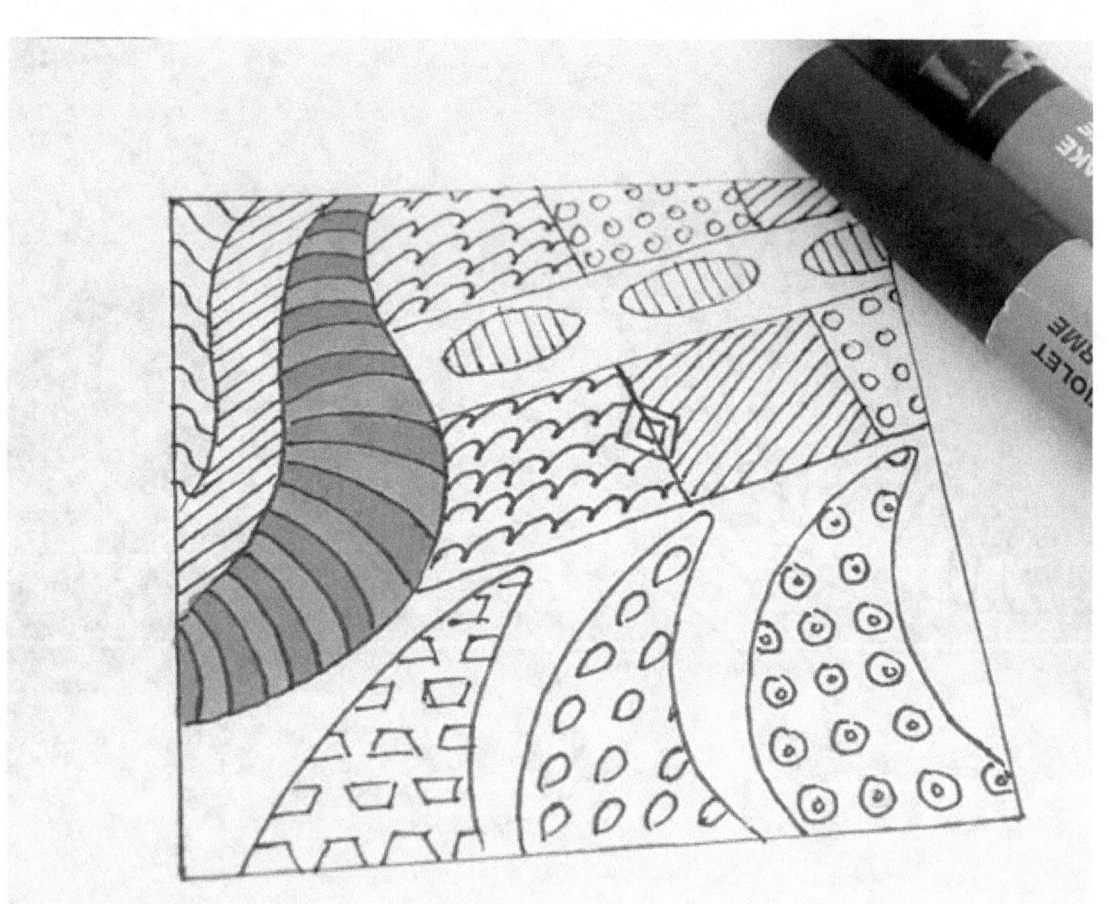

5

Add color or shading as desired.